THE
GARDENS
OF
VENICE
AND THE
VENETO

THE
GARDENS
OF
VENICE
AND THE
VENETO

JENNY CONDIE

PHOTOGRAPHS BY

ALEX RAMSAY

FRANCES LINCOLN PUBLISHERS

CONTENTS

ACKNOWLEDGEMENTS

I would like to express my gratitude to the many people whose generosity, patience and kindness made the research for this book such a pleasurable undertaking. Owners, administrators, caretakers, gardeners, librarians and scholars, each in their own way and very often in several, have contributed their time and expertise to answering my many questions and enlightening me about aspects of their work that I didn't even know to query. To their stewardship is owed the preservation of a unique and fragile heritage and I hope I have done justice to their spectacular efforts.
I should like to extend particular thanks to Fra Agostino, Contessa Anna Guglielmi Barnabò, Francesca Bortolotto Possati, Contessa Marina Emo, Conte Nicolò Giusti del Giardino, Joram Harel, Domenico Luciani, Dott. Giuseppe Marchiori and Signora Raffaella Marchiori, Contessa Francesca Piovene Giusti, Dott. Armando Pizzoni-Ardemani, Dott.ssa Mariella Scalabrin, Dott.ssa Paola Scalella, Dott.ssa Stefania Torresan, and Dott.ssa Alessia Zanandrea. Special thanks are also due to Enrico Palandri, Polly Coles and my editor, Jane Crawley, for their unstinting help, encouragement and support. Finally, I am indebted to Helena Attlee without whose counsel and friendship this book would not have been written.

JENNY CONDIE

My particular thanks to Jenny Condie, without whose diplomacy, determination and charm this book would not exist. I am also deeply grateful to all the Palandri family (great and small) for their boundlessly generous hospitality. And, of course, thanks as ever to all those who make and care for these lovely places.

ALEX RAMSAY

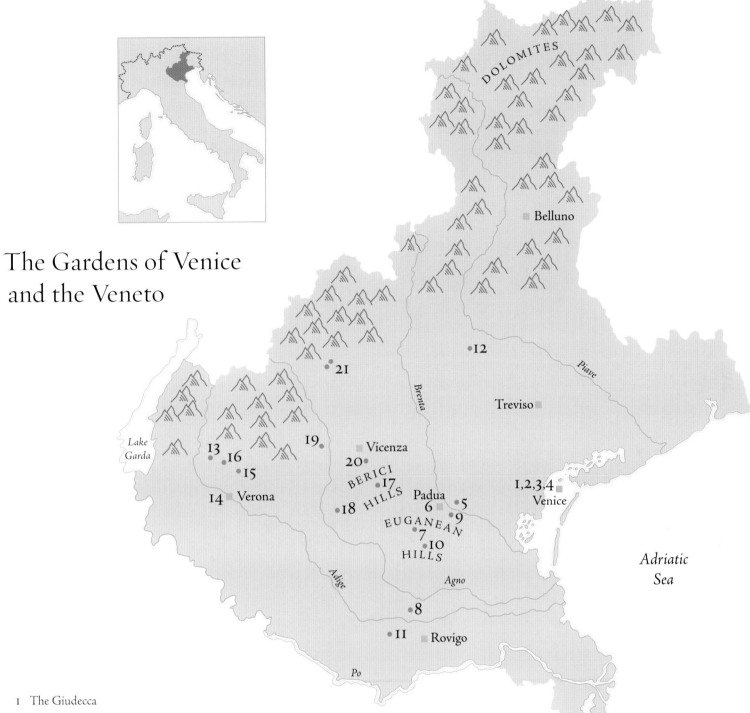

The Gardens of Venice
and the Veneto

Lake Garda

DOLOMITES

Belluno

Piave

Brenta

Treviso

21

12

Vicenza

19

13 16
15

20

17

BERICI
HILLS

Padua
6 5
9

18

EUGANEAN

14 Verona

Adige

7
10
HILLS

8

Agno

*Adriatic
Sea*

1,2,3,4
Venice

11 Rovigo

Po

INTRODUCTION

IN THE SEASON OF DAMP AND BITTER COLD, when Venice withdraws into herself behind drifting banks of grey fog and the melancholic hoots of ships call out to each other across the indistinct waters, an invisible presence creeps over certain crumbling brick walls. It wafts silently down the narrow *calli*, becoming trapped in tiny courtyards or crossing *campi* in the wake of hunched and scurrying figures. Ousting the pervasive stench of stagnant water and sewer, it pools in certain favoured spots or filters narrowly on an air current like a wisp of smoke. Drawn into the nostrils, its light, bright sweetness brings a pang of sudden recognition and a sense of joy. It is the season of wintersweet once more, and from countless invisible gardens across the city, the waxy yellow and amber flowers are releasing their scent on the chill winter air. The associations come crowding in: of slowly lengthening days to Carnival and Lent, and then of other scents to follow, of heavenly sweet box and fragrant loquat, of viburnum and the delicate almond of a *Clematis armandii* by the Accademia bridge. From Venice's hidden gardens a succession of perfumes spill out, presenting a geography of smells and an intangible calendar of the year's cycle to every passer-by.

As spring rushes in, rose blossoms cascade down walls and burst through trellises, window boxes trail fronds down the fronts of buildings, and terraces squeezed between high palazzi are swathed in huge hanging clusters of wisteria. On hundreds of *altane* – little wooden platforms perched precariously on the rooftops – lemon trees and geraniums are carefully unwrapped from their winter coverings and kitchen herbs replenished and repotted. Only at first glance does Venice appear the least green of cities. In fact gardens abound and are treasured, from the dankest private courtyard with its aspidistras and ferns, the still hush of a palazzo garden with its ghostly statuary and gnarled pittosporum, to the sprawling monastery gardens with their ancient vineyards, orchards and vegetable plots. The closely-built nature of the urban fabric means that no garden is experienced solely by its owners but contributes its weft of colours, forms and scents to the dense warp of brick and stone, enriching the cityscape for all.

Selecting the gardens to include in this volume has not been pain-free: there have been not a few agonising choices and many niggling doubts. Estimates as to the number of *ville venete* alone are in the region of 4,000, and almost all of these have, at one time or another, had a garden. The great majority have of course been lost, but a remarkable number have survived, a feat all the more extraordinary considering that the region has at various times been invaded and bombed, suffered frequent and extensive

LEFT A gondolier turns down Rio de San Trovaso from the Grand Canal.
RIGHT After their introduction to the Veneto in the latter half of the sixteenth century, citrus plants became one of the main adornments for gardens.

flooding, social upheaval, and has undergone, over the past forty years or so, an economic transformation that has changed vast tracts of countryside into urban sprawl, also described in more accommodating terms as *città diffusa*. The particularity of the Veneto's varied geography – from the Alpine chain in the north, to the vast plain stretching towards the Adriatic sea with its flood-prone rivers and outcrops of geologically diverse hills – and the vivacity of its cities, notwithstanding (but also thanks to) their proximity to Venice, have endowed the region with a unique beauty and diversity that is nowhere expressed as limpidly and magnificently as in its great gardens.

Sometimes, in conversations with owners and gardeners encountered during the research for this book, the slightest hint of an antique hostility towards Venice has been

The search for light and space drives many plants to scramble out from their frequently narrow confines. Here a wisteria offers its colour and perfume to the *calle* beyond the garden wall.

discernible, a relic of what must for long centuries have been a bitter grudge against that once mighty power which lorded it over all her mainland territories. Such traces of antipathy, now so superfluous – for who could be resentful today of the tiny, water-bound city that cannot even defend herself from the friendly fire of mass tourism? – have been useful reminders of how enormously the balance of power has changed in this region and of how long in folk memory ancient resentments can linger. Venice still exerts a cultural and political hegemony over the region of which she is capital, is still the main point of reference for the people of the Veneto, and will undoubtedly remain the main destination for the visitor bound for this part of the world. Echoes of her unique style of architecture are to be found all over the region, and many of those responsible for shaping the Veneto landscape and its gardens first opened their eyes upon her courtyards and canals.

Since gardens may be said to be the expression of man's striving to reconcile his physical and spiritual needs in the corner of the natural world in which he finds himself, it will be all the more enlightening to touch briefly on the reasons why people should have chosen to settle in this most unpromising of environments in the first place. They came, so the story goes, from the highly civilised urban centres of the northern Adriatic, cities of the Roman empire such as Oderzo, Altino, Eraclea and Aquilea which, from the early fifth century A D, were increasingly subjected to attacks by invading barbarians from northeastern Europe. The nearby lagoon which had provided these populations with salt and fish and whose unpredictable shallows they knew how to navigate, became first a refuge, and then, as successive waves of invaders continued to lay waste to the mainland, a home. The fragile nature of the early Venetians' existence in a watery world and their initial sense of impermanence is reflected in the word still used to denote the Venetian mainland: *terraferma*, land that is still, that does not move. A tidal lagoon is above all a dynamic, unstable environment, the contours of which are continually being moulded and reshaped according to the vagaries of wave and current. This immense area of marsh, mudflats and shallow, brackish water in the northern reaches of the Adriatic was created when sediments from the rivers pouring into the coastal area built up deposits that eventually formed barriers to the sea, and behind which fresh water became trapped. Regularly flushed out by the ebb and flow of seawater through gaps in the barrier, it was, and is, a singularly rich yet delicate environment, demanding a series of unique adaptations on the part of all the living organisms, including humans, that inhabit it.

In time, techniques were developed to make living on the islands viable and even productive. Establishing a supply of fresh drinking water must have been among the first priorities and the richly ornamented well-heads in the squares, courtyards and, later, the gardens of the city are a reminder of how important was the overcoming of this problem. The consolidation of the muddy margins of the islands was another pressing necessity, but here man's interventions were not always successful, as the shrinking and disappearance of some of them testifies. The constant

incursions of briny water made the growing of food plants along the shores difficult, but on higher ground further into the interiors of the islands, certain plants were found to grow well. These spaces, called *campi*, or fields, were kept free of buildings in order to grow crops and keep livestock, and were only later paved over to become today's city squares, their original purpose now only discernible in their name. The convention developed whereby dwellings were situated right on the edge of the water with the boat moored at the door, while behind, set back from the canal, were the paved courtyards for the collection of rainwater and beyond that, a further space for cultivation. This basic layout, dictated by purely practical concerns, would continue, with very little variation, to inform Venetian domestic architecture for centuries to come.

As the city grew and its trade with the eastern Mediterranean prospered, spices became one of the major sources of revenue, shipped from as far away as Persia, India and even China. As a result of this, and of the burgeoning commerce in medicinal plants that it engendered, private botanical gardens proliferated in Venice. One of the most remarkable was that owned by Pietro Antonio Michiel at San Trovaso, described as being, 'as remarkable for the rare plants to be found there as for the aqueducts and precious grotesques made with admirable art which are also to be seen'. Between 1553 and 1565, Michiel, who corresponded with botanists all over Italy and abroad, produced the encyclopedic *I cinque libri di piante*, a five-volume manuscript of all known plants, testifying to the huge variety of plant material circulating in Venice at the time. The most tangible result of all this ferment was the founding, in 1545, of the ORTO BOTANICO DI PADOVA, an enterprise in which several Venetians played a decisive role.

The Renaissance revitalisation of culture and knowledge that began in central Italy spread to Venice during the fifteenth and sixteenth centuries, promoting a renewed interest in antiquity and investing all branches of learning. The cultural climate was such that many botanical gardens became meeting places for members of literary, artistic and humanist circles. From the descriptions that have survived

Community allotments, like the new Bio Orto Angelo Raffaele, run jointly by the Council and a historic gardens club, have encouraged interest in the city's horticultural past and are a prized amenity for local people.

of these 'places of delight', no trace of which, sadly, remains today, a picture emerges of the same collector's mania that governed plant choice being applied to inanimate features such as rocks, shells, corals and assorted curiosities. One famous garden on the Giudecca contained a colonnade, fountains, a frescoed loggia and a grotto decorated with pumice stone and Murano glass. This fascination for the exotic and the esoteric was by no means confined to Venice: two mainland gardens of around the same period, GIARDINO GIUSTI in Verona and VILLA DELLA TORRE at Fumane in the region of Valpolicella, conceived, in their different ways, as homages to the classical world, also featured elaborate grottoes, in which illusionistic devices were combined with elements from the marine or subterranean worlds in order to elicit a sense of wonderment tinged by fear in the unsuspecting visitor.

The native frugality of the necessarily self-sufficient islander was deeply rooted in the Venetian consciousness, so that, however erudite or entertaining the garden, there was sure to be plenty of space dedicated also to the more pragmatic activity of growing foodstuffs. The presence in the garden of a *brolo*, or orchard, a vine pergola and rows of beans was considered no less noble for being utilitarian.

This pride in being able to live on the produce of the lagoon is still very much alive today, with market stalls loudly proclaiming the local (*nostrano*) origin of certain vegetables. The large island of Sant'Erasmo in the north lagoon is a patchwork of market gardens and small-holdings, and has made a speciality out of growing a small, purple-headed variety of artichoke.

If the island of the Giudecca was the original market garden of Venice, it shared the primacy for the greatest number of patrician villas and gardens with the island of Murano. Despite the presence of the glass furnaces, relocated there for safety reasons in 1295, some of Venice's most magnificent country residences were built on Murano during the fifteenth and sixteenth centuries. Their fashionable gardens, known only from contemporary descriptions, set new standards of intellectual refinement, but it was not long before the more spacious *terraferma* exerted its siren call and the gardens and their owners migrated to more salubrious and rural territory.

Vineyards in the monastery of the Discalced Carmelite Friars, where birdsong competes with the tannoy system from the railway station next door. The medicinal herb *Dracocephalum moldavicum* was once grown and distilled here.

ABOVE The garden of the Franciscan monastery of the Redentore on the Giudecca is overlooked by ancient cypresses.
BELOW Woodcut from the *Hypnerotomachia Poliphili*, an illustrated allegorical romance published in Venice in 1499 and a rich source of information about the architectural and botanical elements of the gardens of the period.

Convents and monasteries were very numerous both on the islands scattered about the lagoon and in the main part of the city too, and they often had extensive gardens at their disposal. In 1494 the Milanese writer and ecclesiast Pietro Casola passed through Venice on his way to Jerusalem, and amidst his general astonishment at the city's beauty and richness, he wrote of how, 'I admired nothing so much in this city built upon water as the sight of so many beautiful gardens, in particular those of all the religious orders'. Some of these gardens, or *orti*, are still tended by religious communities of nuns and monks who carry on the work of their predecessors, digging and planting, earthing up potatoes, harvesting grapes and olives, pruning fruit trees and rearing chickens, just a wall's thickness away from the heaving throngs of visitors traipsing through the crowded city streets. Screened by pink brick and centuries-old cypress trees, their different order still holds.

The fourteenth-century house and garden of the poet Francesco Petrarca at Arquà in the Euganean hills near Padua is often cited as a precursor of the vogue for villa

The temple-like Villa Emo at Rivella, by Vincenzo Scamozzi. Palladio and his followers invented a type of country house – the 'casa di villa' – that was unique to the Veneto and to the needs of a new landowning class.

building that began in earnest during the early years of the sixteenth century. The ideal model of life that Petrarch represented, far from the dirt and strife of the city, surrounded by books and friends and intent on improving his land, clearly echoed similar descriptions by classical writers such as Pliny the Younger, and would in time exert its appeal on certain members of the Venetian nobility. Already by the early fifteenth century, Venice had expanded her dominion to include the whole of the region now known as the Veneto, as well as parts of Lombardy to the west and Friuli to the east. A century later, this hegemony was challenged by the Papal States which, together with all the major European superpowers, formed the League of Cambrai. Venice lost territory during the Italian Wars that resulted, only to win most of it back in 1516, but then it was the turn of the Ottoman Empire to threaten her prosperity. In response to increasing tensions in her seaward empire, the Venetian Republic began to invest heavily in her landward possessions, setting in motion a vast programme of public works aimed at increasing cultivable land and improving the transport network by deviating rivers and cutting canals. Former merchants who had made fortunes in shipping, trading and banking poured their money into their country estates. Being canny businessmen, they understood the necessity of 'living over the shop' but they wanted to do so in style: thus the villa Veneto was born.

Many of Palladio's villas were built in response to just such a need. They were sited at the centre of the property and slightly elevated from their surroundings in order to ensure panoramic views as well as to confer dignity on their occupants. Their grandeur came not from their scale, which was usually modest, but from their harmonious proportions. Palladio wrote almost nothing about the arrangement of gardens around his villas, with the sole exception of VILLA BARBARO at Maser. His follower, Vincenzo Scamozzi, was much more prescriptive, and some of his ideas have been reinstated in the garden surrounding the late sixteenth-century VILLA EMO at Rivella near Monselice. This twentieth-century creation, refreshingly tongue-in-cheek, has taken Scamozzi's rather pompous conception of a formally laid-out forecourt with geometrical parterre and transformed it by the addition (in clipped box) of the owners' initials intertwined, but in a free-flowing and funky script of the 1960s. Elsewhere in this garden, dogs' graves are solemnly marked by groups of antique-style columns, and the nameless statues at either end of the poplar avenue are known affectionately as Doris Day and Errol Flynn.

During the sixteenth century, as the *terraferma* began for the first time in Venice's history to look like the best hope for her survival, stewardship of the land became a vital concern. 'Santa agricoltura' had been the byword proclaimed by the Venetian statesman and agricultural treatise writer Alvise Corner (1484–1566) who had exhorted his countrymen to look to the land rather than the sea for sustenance, and many took him at his word. Its importance is evident in the iconographical pro-grammes designed for villa gardens, in which pagan deities connected with agriculture, hunting and water sources mingle with allegorical figures representing such virtues as peace, concord and prosperity. The complexity of some of these schemes was a function of the erudition of the classical scholars, men of letters, artists and architects who congregated in the houses of the new landowners. Unlike the gardens of central Italy, those of the Veneto, which tended to be attached to working farms, did not involve large-scale landscaping, and exploited instead those features of the landscape that already existed, whether hilltops and gentle slopes, springs or canals.

A smell of byre and straw dust still seems to float up from the pages of records detailing the acquisitions of land and the laborious wrangles over access to springs in the protracted gestation of the garden of VILLA BARBARIGO at Valsanzibio, one of the Veneto's most extravagantly beautiful gardens. Quibbles over workmen's bills, lawsuits and legal battles, claims and counter-claims made by legitimate and natural offspring rustle down the centuries in a shuffling of papers, a tying up of bundles, a thump of judge's hammer on the bench. The garden has come down to us, however, almost unscathed, though there is polemic in some quarters about the height of the hedges. Meanwhile its biologist owner is fighting off tree viruses with ingenious contraptions of his own design and struggling to replace the four-hundred-year-old hydraulic systems that feed the much-loved water tricks, a rarity in the Veneto.

In the quite different context of Valpolicella, the baroque magnificence of VILLA ALLEGRI ARVEDI'S parterre terrace seems to proclaim confidence in the bounty of the soil and a determination to wrest more than food from its rich tilth. The spirit of the place bursts through in the rhythmic patterns of box, yew and persimmon as they cascade down the slope from the villa. The tall brick chimney that pokes up from the adjacent farm buildings is a proud symbol of past enterprise, without which this garden might not have survived. Another type of might is manifested in the long straight line that slices through the rich farmland of the Basso Vicentino at VILLA FRACANZAN PIOVENE. The process of restoring an historical garden, which is still underway here, has been movingly recorded by the

Villa Allegri Arvedi in the Valpolicella is a working farm in which beauty and utility are combined to striking effect. Many villas and gardens in the Veneto have maintained strong agricultural ties throughout the intervening centuries.

present owner and reminds us how these gardens are not simply historical artefacts that belong to our common history (though they are that as well), but places invested with multiple and intimate meanings for those who were brought up in them and often look after them still.

Many villas were built on pre-existing fortified structures which could be exploited for their site. At VILLA TRISSINO, the architect Francesco Muttoni toiled for a number of years to convert a castle keep with an adjacent jutting plug of rock into a villa and garden of great beauty and complexity that offered multiple panoramic views of the surrounding valleys. On the unremittingly flat plain between Venice and Padua, commanding views of this kind were unthinkable, so different techniques were employed. At the sumptuous VILLA PISANI at Stra, for example, elevated viewing galleries were built in order to maximise appreciation of the meticulously planned perspectival views. In addition, a series of *claires-voies* or wrought-iron windows and gates in the exterior walls extended the vistas into the surrounding countryside. In 1728 Montesquieu made the journey from Venice to Padua in the famous *burchiello*, a luxury, horse-drawn barge plying the banks of the Brenta Canal that connected the two cities. 'There are beautiful houses belonging to the nobility', he noted. 'The nobleman Pisani has begun one that will be extraordinarily lofty, but only the exterior sections have been completed and from along the banks of the river one can see magnificent gateways

that will lead onto the avenues of the enormous park created here on the Brenta, in deliberate imitation of the gardens of our Royal palaces.'

Lined by a succession of splendid villas mirrored in its waters, the Riviera del Brenta, as it became known, was the rural continuation of the Grand Canal. By the eighteenth century it had become the favoured destination for the *villeggiatura* of the Venetian nobility, those periods in the summer and autumn months when they moved out of Venice *en masse* to enjoy the fresh air and space of the countryside. In 1739 the ever-curious French traveller and writer Charles de Brosses resolved to take the *burchiello* and visit all the new villas, but gave up because there were simply too many. It was the same story all along the

LEFT Villa Trissino Marzotto, Trissino. The statues around the pond and along the balustrade surrounding the garden of the lower villa were executed by Orazio Marinali and his workshop, a well-organised Veneto family business that supplied villa owners with high quality garden sculpture in local stone.
ABOVE An engraving from Gianfrancesco Costa, *Delle Delizie del fiume Brenta*, Venice, 1750–62. A *burchiello* arrives at Villa Pisani Barbarigo where the *broderie* parterre stretches all the way down to the banks of the canal.
RIGHT Villa Barbarigo Pizzoni Ardemani at Valsanzibio, one of Italy's great Baroque gardens. A spectacular watergate is reflected in the pool by the roadside, recalling the Venetian origins of the family responsible for its creation.

terraglio too, the main road between Venice and Treviso. 'The innocent enjoyment of the countryside has become a passion these days, a mania, a riot', wrote the Venetian playwright Carlo Goldoni in the preface to his comic *Villeggiatura* trilogy which satirised the vogue. In the decadent atmosphere of the final years of the Republic, the *villeggiatura* lost any agricultural connotations it might have had and became a society duty in which the participants were expected to indulge in much conspicuous consumption. And whereas originally the desire for peaceful retirement in some *locus amoenus* had been inspired by the poetry of such venerable ancients as Virgil, 'Now, on the other hand', continued the playwright ruefully, 'ambition has penetrated the forests: holiday-makers bring with them into the countryside all the pomp and uproar of the cities and they have poisoned the happiness of the country people'.

Families competed with each other to offer extravagant feasts, concerts, balls and parties, in a final flourish of Venetian magnificence. The most fashionable gardens incorporated such elements of the French style as *tapis verts*, *berceaux*, and *broderie* parterres in addition to the more traditionally Italian sculptures and citrus plants in terracotta pots. Gardens were expected to host large-scale entertainments, concerts and plays, and these required the installation of stages and backdrops. Sometimes these were permanent structures, such as the loggia at the bottom of the garden of PALAZZO SORANZO CAPPELLO in Venice. In the countryside there was room to be more extravagant, even to the point of constructing a private theatre in the villa itself, as at Villa Widmann at Bagnoli di Sopra near Padua, where Goldoni was frequently a guest and performed as an actor. Only traces of all this former magnificence are visible today, but a splendid green theatre, carved from box, yew and hornbeam and dating from the end of the eighteenth century, is still in use in the GIARDINO DI POJEGA at Villa Rizzardi, near Verona.

Allegorical statues, in overt celebration of the virtues and munificence of an aristocratic elite that in the Veneto was enjoying a period of unprecedented peace and prosperity, poured out of local sculptors' workshops. More often than not their designs were still based on prototypes in printed manuals such as Cesare Ripa's useful *Iconologia*,

LEFT Giardino di Pojega at Villa Rizzardi near Verona. The final act of the Venetian drama played out, for some, in an endless round of entertainment in sumptuous surroundings. Few gardens, however, boasted a green theatre on the scale of Count Antonio Rizzardi's. RIGHT Ca' Dolfin-Marchiori, Lendinara. The vogue for the English landscape garden swept through the Veneto in the nineteenth century, creating an uncharacteristically sombre mood and leaving many statues picturesquely strewn on the ground.

first published in Rome in 1593. As the eighteenth century wore on, however, such statues were increasingly likely to be accompanied or even replaced by genre figures, such as peasant girls, exotic 'types', rustics, theatrical players, or even dwarves, as at VILLA VALMARANA AI NANI on the outskirts of Vicenza. Some gardens of this period attempted to recapture the more sober spirit of the past, giving rise to complex reconstructions of the earlier style of *giardino all'italiana*, such as that carried out at VILLA TRENTO DA SCHIO at Costozza. A similar historicising impulse was at work in twentieth-century Venice. The rose-filled garden of PALAZZO CAPPELLO MALIPIERO BARNABÒ was designed in the 1950s, yet its forms recall the lost eighteenth-century gardens of Venice's decadence, imbuing the canal-side plot with a feeling of nostalgia for a long-gone world.

The importation to England of the classically-inspired Palladian villa coincided with the development of a new and distinctive informal garden style, the most famous proponents of which were William Kent and later, Lancelot 'Capability' Brown. Although this new type of landscape garden was readily accepted into many parts of northern Europe and hailed as a brilliant interpretation of the spirit of the times, its entry into Italy was slower and more arduous. The philosophical implications of the *giardino all'inglese* taxed the intellect of an erudite group of scholars and theorists in the Veneto, some of whom had gardens of their own. To Horace Walpole's arrogant

assertion, 'We have given the true model of gardening to the world', they responded by holding a series of public debates on the subject in Padua between 1792 and 1798, being only temporarily interrupted by the arrival of the French Grande Armée and the end of the Republic of Venice.

The more enthusiastic proponents of the new style tended to be Anglophiles – men such as Melchiorre Cesarotti (1732–1808), the translator of James Macpherson's *The Works of Ossian* and Thomas Gray's *Elegy Written in a Country Churchyard*, who referred to his literary-inspired garden at Selvazzano near Padua as his *'poema vegetale'*. Sadly, this and other philosophical and meditative gardens of the period have not survived. But the potential inherent in the idea of the garden as a sentimental landscape, or as a visualisation of different states of mind was not lost on a young architect called Giuseppe Jappelli who, more than any other designer of his time, left the imprint of the English or Romantic garden on the Veneto. Through the agency of Jappelli, the *villa veneta* finally ceased to have any agricultural pretensions. His masonic garden, built over a number of years at Saonara in the grounds of VILLA VALMARANA (then known as VILLA CITTADELLA-VIGODARZERE), with its elements of mystery and surprise, was one of the strangest creations of its time. Perhaps because he had also worked as a scenographer, Jappelli's style had great impact and spawned a number of imitators, often of the amateur variety. It is not recorded what, if anything, Domenico Marchiori owed to the older architect when he conceived his own garden some years later at CA' DOLFIN-MARCHIORI in Lendinara, a poetic reverie in which the visitor was guided through a series of scenic set pieces, distant both in time and place.

Lost worlds, hints of ruined civilisations, an eclectic tendency to include picturesque elements of distant cultures, these were the major themes of the mid-nineteenth-century Romantic Veneto garden. The rush to convert at least part of formerly grand villa gardens laid out in the French or Italian style, with their labour-intensive parterres, *tapis verts* and pleached alleys, into more 'natural' English-style land-scape gardens, was partly attributable to an understandable desire on the part of owners to contain costs. But a century and a half later, the problems inherent in maintaining a *giardino all'inglese* in the Veneto climate, with its extremes

of temperature, frequent typhoons and infestations of
fast-growing species such as bay laurel and false acacia, are
often only too sadly evident. Informal woodlands planted
with tall-growing species of trees have fallen victim to
disease or frost or have simply reached the limits of their
lifespan, making costly programmes of tree felling and
replanting obligatory. Such interventions are often beyond
the budget of private owners, with the result that many
gardens of this type have reverted to impenetrable thickets,
havens at least for wildlife but barely legible any longer as
artefacts. To compound their problems of survival, the
intrinsic ephemerality of the architectural components that
gave these gardens meaning has rendered them particularly
susceptible to the passage of time. Building materials such
as brick and the first experiments in cast concrete have
proved no match for the picturesque but damaging effects
of moss and ivy, or the underground turbulence caused
by tree roots, so that many fake ruins are now true ruins,
presenting challenging difficulties for restorers. Those
gardens that relied for their effect on the introduction of
exotic species have seen their *raison d'être* undermined over
the last fifty years, as garden centres have put non-native
species at the disposal of anybody with a balcony or a
space to fill between the garage and the front door. The
novelty value and aesthetic appeal of such nineteenth-
century exotics as Japanese laurel, privet and aspidistra
have long faded, and the dense shrubberies containing
them have a gloomy quality that was never intended
at their inception. In 1862, when the GIARDINO
JACQUARD opened its gates to the factory workers of
Schio, colour was rampant, and hosts of exotic trees and
flowers were part of the planned entertainment, forming
a sensational botanical backdrop to the part-didactic,
part-amusement-park atmosphere conjured by its architect,
Antonio Caregaro Negrin, a former pupil of Jappelli at
the Venetian Accademia di Belle Arti.

An outstanding example of the potential for invention
and innovation offered by the fusion of national garden
styles is the garden of VILLA PISANI AT VESCOVANA.
Unlike most of the gardens in this volume, Vescovana
was not designed by a professional architect but by
a woman – and a foreign woman at that. Turkish by
birth, Anglo-Dutch and French by descent and Italian by
adoption, Evelina van Millingen married into the Venetian
aristocracy and found herself managing, in the latter half
of the nineteenth century, an unpromising acreage of
sullen clay on the Po plain. Behind the villa at the centre of
the farm she combined the various strands of her cultural
origins into a sensual and romantic garden that is as richly
fascinating as her life story. Her example continues to
inspire the present owner, also a woman and an outsider,
to persist with the selfless act of love that is looking after
an historic garden. The survival of this intriguing example
of a Victorian Italianate garden in Italy is thus, for the
time being, ensured.

Many of the visitors to Vescovana would also have
been familiar with another famous garden created by a
foreigner, this time in Venice. In its heyday at the turn of
the nineteenth and twentieth centuries, the EDEN garden
on the Giudecca must have been one of the most visited
gardens in Venice, and was certainly one of the most
admired. Scarcely a literary or artistic personage visiting
Venice went away without setting foot at least once in
its hospitable courtyard or under its long vine pergolas
running tantalisingly towards the mirror-like surface of
the south lagoon. Sadly it is no longer to be visited, but
it does still exist, and its story is by no means over.

Meanwhile, during the brief periods of French rule that
had followed Napoleon's invasion of the Veneto in 1797,
Venice had been subjected to a wide-ranging programme
of modernisation that included urban planning on
an unprecedented and quite foreign scale. Never in her
thousand-year history had the Republic of Venice enter-
tained the idea of providing green space for its citizens, but
the new rulers ordained that among other groundbreaking
changes to the status quo, two new gardens were to be
built: a royal garden at St Mark's Square for the use of
the Viceroy of Italy and his family, and a public garden
at the far eastern end of the city, in the poorer *sestiere*
of Castello. Several churches were among the buildings
demolished to make way for a grandiose scheme that
included barracks, stables for horses and parade grounds,
in the full expectation that Venice would adopt the ways
of imperial France. The Riva degli Schiavoni was widened
in order to provide a long promenade between St Mark's
Square and the eastern end of the city, from which
panoramic views of the south lagoon and the basin of
St Mark's could be enjoyed.

The plans were drawn up by Gian Antonio Selva, a renowned Venetian architect who had rebuilt the city's La Fenice opera house in neo-classical style. Planned to consist of two segments, with formal and geometrically organised beds at the entrance and a landscaped area at the eastern extremity, planted with informal groupings of trees rising to a small hill with a pavilion on top (now, appropriately, hosting British art during the Venice Art Biennale), the gardens were to have been provided with various amenities including a public bathing station, a beer-hall, café and restaurant. Lack of funds meant that many of these plans were shelved, in addition to which the gardens were at first widely resented and little used. In 1887

Giardino Jacquard, Schio. The box hedge of the *giardino all'italiana* is readmitted in curvilinear form, lending stability and grace to Caregaro Negrin's richly eclectic composition.

part of the grounds were taken over for the Esposizione Nazionale Artistica, an art exhibition that later became the Biennale. National pavilions for the showcasing of art works were built and about two-thirds of the former public garden was made off-limits except by payment of an entrance fee during the Biennale, which now alternates yearly with the Architecture Biennale. The park is planted with a rich variety of trees, some of which are of great age: giant planes, cypresses, poplars, limes and the gaunt trunks of *Celtis australis* form a backdrop to the decorative forms of magnolia, palm, golden rain tree, pittosporum, carob and olive. The effects of the different foliages through the seasons are perhaps best appreciated from a moving boat, where, like their architectural equivalents on the Grand Canal, they can be seen processing in a spectacular display of colour and texture. Although the citizenry is now

reconciled to this 'foreign' amenity, a failure on the part of the city authorities to maintain the gardens to a high standard contributes to the sense of an imposed public works programme that did not quite make the grade.

The Napoleonic suppression of religious institutions greatly reduced the numbers of convents and monasteries in the city and put an end to the life of many of the smaller islands. For San Giorgio Maggiore, the island directly opposite the Ducal Palace, French rule resulted in the loss of many of its movable artistic treasures, but the Palladian church with its magisterial cloisters remained. The twentieth-century conversion of most of the monastery buildings into a centre for academic research – the Fondazione Giorgio Cini – has ensured a continuity of use that is rare in the Venetian archipelago, and indeed, the island continues to grow and its amenities to expand.

A labyrinth, arranged in the shape of an open book and dedicated to the memory of the Argentinian writer Jorge Luis Borges, was unveiled in 2011.

In the north of the city, two more public gardens were opened during the twentieth century, both on the site of formerly grand private gardens. The Parco Savorgnan is a huge, tree-filled amenity just metres away from one of the busiest and shabbiest city thoroughfares, while at the Parco Fondazione Groggia, picturesque ruins and Art Nouveau greenhouse share the grounds with a small and thriving theatre. The gardens of Sant'Elena, Venice's version of a garden city, built on the ruins of a failed late-nineteenth-century industrial park, offer informal sporting facilities and scenic views of the city's cupolas between rows of stone pines.

'Venice is not a museum!' runs a popular slogan, coined by locals frustrated by the onerous presence of so many tourists. While living a normal life certainly poses a number of unique problems, the question of how to respond creatively to a city so rich in the artefacts of the past has a special urgency for artists and architects. In the case of gardens, however, Carlo Scarpa's contribution at the FONDAZIONE QUERINI STAMPALIA bears comparison with anything that the ancient city has to offer, apart from age. It is a quietly understated masterpiece that combines, in miniature, traditional Venetian garden elements with high-quality artisanship and an oriental sense of serene detachment. Fifty years after its conception, its message seems more than ever relevant.

Others have explored the fascinating subject of hidden or private gardens; our leading criterion has been present accessibility – born from the conviction that no picture or story could possibly equate with experiencing these gardens for oneself. Although Alex Ramsay and I have both attempted, in our different ways, to get in close, it is our hope that, beguiled by these pages, the reader will undertake the rest of the journey in person.

LEFT The garden culture of Venice and the Veneto informed the work of Carlo Scarpa, and can be seen throughout his design for the Fondazione Querini Stampalia.
RIGHT The twenty-first century labyrinth behind the cloisters of San Giorgio Maggiore was inspired by Borges' short story 'The Garden of Forking Paths' and based on a design by Randoll Coate.

VENICE

THE GIUDECCA

L'ISOLA DELLE FOCHE – THE ISLE OF SEALS, as it is rather disparagingly called by Venetians – lies to the south of the main body of Venice, echoing the city's curving forms in a minor key. Its sinuous, fish-like shape perhaps suggested its original name of Spinalonga, or long fish bone, but later, for reasons that are still disputed, it became known as the Giudecca. The island has a reputation for being a cold place, home to a hardy race of islanders with their own weather-beaten ways. From a distance, its long, north-facing façade of buildings looks elegant, but on stepping ashore, the surroundings are suddenly bleak: greenish water slops wetly up and over the *fondamenta* and runs in a dark stain towards the shops that line the waterfront. On a cold winter's day the narrow shoreline is an inhospitable place, blasted by winds that have gathered speed and moisture as they power across the open lagoon from the northeast. From the marrow-freezing sunlessness of this wet, grey place one looks out across a stretch of choppy water to the south-facing, sun-drenched Zattere and further off to the right, the dazzling lacework of the Ducal Palace and the cupolas of St Mark's. Over there, orchestras are playing and children are chasing pigeons in the sun, while here people stand in line at the fishmonger's stamping their chilblained toes in their boots. It seems unfair, it seems like the island that fortune forgot, forever condemned to struggle against the sea squall.

But this is only half the story. As soon as you enter one of the narrow *calli* that lead away from the shore towards the island's interior, the wind drops, and a series of homely little *campi* opens out, criss-crossed by the usual washing

lines and animated by the usual tinkling of forks and pot lids. This is how certain parts of Venice must have looked for centuries: grass and weeds sprouting outside the door, fishing nets slung out to dry, bits of boats leaning against the walls and children darting and scuffling between the houses. Before long the other side of the island is reached, announcing itself in glimpses of bright water at the end of long, narrow alleyways or beyond flower-crammed court-yards. Suddenly, all is warmth and light, the sun-baked bricks radiate in south-facing walls and the undisturbed waters of the south lagoon shimmer for as far as the eye can see under a huge sky. The contrast with the north shore could not be more marked.

In recent years the Giudecca has undergone the kind of changes that would be unimaginable in central Venice: the

LEFT Iceberg roses in the garden of the Bauer Palladio Hotel, once the garden of the convent attached to the Church of the Zitelle.
RIGHT Makeshift shade in the IRE garden, formerly part of the Zitelle convent grounds. The word for shade – *ombra* – also means a glass of wine.

conversion of churches, monasteries, factories and ware-houses into mainly public housing and much new building on the island's south side has transformed a formerly dingy and dilapidated environment into an urban neighbourhood with a very contemporary feel. It has not always been so. Whereas Venice grew tightly around her churches and *campi*, the island of the Giudecca remained for centuries a country cousin, with extensive vegetable plots and orchards providing fruit and vegetables to the growing city. Jacopo de' Barbari's famous woodcut bird's-eye view of Venice, published in 1500, shows part of the island in fascinating detail, with monasteries and fine houses ranged along the north shore, their gardens extending all the way to the south lagoon. Neat rows of vegetables, fruit trees and vine pergolas are enclosed by a network of walls and wattle fences, beyond which remain areas of uncultivated ground. The Giudecca was then still relatively underpopulated, a decisive factor for Michelangelo Buonarroti who took refuge here in 1529 '*per vivere solitario*' (to live in solitude) while he worked on his (unsuccessful) designs for the new Rialto Bridge. This very quality of restfulness recommended it to Venetian patricians anxious to leave the suffocating heat and closeness of their palazzi in the

city centre, and long before it became fashionable for the rich to build summer residences further afield on the mainland and along the banks of the Brenta Canal, many were content to spend their summers closer to home on suburban Giudecca.

In the nineteenth century the island became the hub of Venice's industrial revolution and factories such as the Molino Stucky flour mill, the Junghans clock factory and the Dreher brewery were built. Many of the pleasure gardens, market gardens, vineyards and orchards disappeared and the Giudecca lost its rural identity for ever, although older locals still remember taking their kitchen scraps to pig owners and chickens scratching in every courtyard until well into the 1950s. Yet pockets of horticultural activity do still survive, evidence of a remarkable continuity of use that has lasted well over five centuries. One variation on the theme of the antique Venetian *brolo* is to be found in the unlikely surroundings of the Hotel Cipriani, an elite hotel built near the site of

BELOW Detail of a woodcut by Jacopo de' Barbari, *Bird's-eye view of Venice*, showing walled gardens and uncultivated land.
RIGHT The boathouse of the Redentore on the Giudecca's southern shore, with part of the monastery garden on either side.

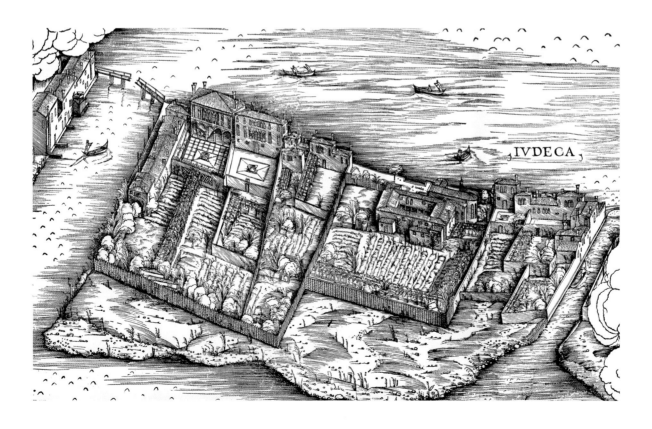

one of the Giudecca's most renowned disappeared gardens, the Palazzo Nani, which once hosted an Academy of Philosophy and Botany founded by Ermolao Barbaro. Behind the ornamental pool in the main landscaped garden, with its pergolas and statuary, and on the other side of a long avenue of magnificent plane trees that forms the backbone of the garden, is a walled vegetable plot, vineyard and orchard, beautifully tended and of considerable size. The vegetables, which are raised organically, are used in the hotel's kitchens, which also make good use of a large herb garden planted chequerboard-style directly outside their noisy premises.

One of the oldest gardens in continuous cultivation is that of the Capuchin Friars Minor of the Church of the Redentore. The Order was already present here in 1576, when the end of a devastating plague prompted the Senate to dedicate a new church to the Redentore (the Redeemer) in gratitude. When it was consecrated in 1592, the friars found themselves guardians of an architectural masterpiece by Andrea Palladio in dazzling white Istrian stone. But the monastery behind, by contrast, is plain and brick-built, with unvarnished pine doors and terracotta-tiled floors worn by the passage of many sandalled feet. It is built around two sides of an extensive and productive monastery garden that extends southward to the old sea wall, where an entry gate from the lagoon with its characteristic *cavana*, or boathouse, straddles the canal.

The garden is arranged in rectangular strips running from north to south and is bound on the eastern wall by a row of some two dozen ancient cypresses that, as well as acting as a windbreak, confer a majestic and ageless solemnity on the place. The resident monks are few nowadays and the vineyard was regretfully abandoned some years ago to save on labour. One pergola remains, supporting eating grapes and an over-productive kiwi.

The microclimate on this side of the Giudecca is such that olive trees thrive, and the monks have a grove big enough to make their own oil, although the olives have to be sent to the mainland for pressing. As well as feeding their novitiates, the monks also provide daily meals to those in need. The long narrow vegetable patch is rotated to provide vegetables all year round. Courgettes, onions, tomatoes, cabbage, aubergines, several varieties of beans: there seems nothing they cannot grow in this naturally fertile, sandy terrain. The artichokes have their own patch and usually a large area is dedicated to pumpkins, a winter staple in these parts. The central orchard area is well supplied with plums, cherries, pears and pomegranates, while down by

ABOVE Olive trees in the Redentore monastery garden, recalling the Umbrian landscape of Assisi, birthplace of St Francis.
RIGHT Orchard, vineyard and neat rows of vegetables in the garden of the Hotel Cipriani on the Giudecca.
FAR RIGHT Eating grapes are all that remain of the Franciscan monastery's once-extensive vineyard at the Redentore.

the henhouse, in an association redolent of the Veneto farmstead, grows a glossy-leaved *Ziziphus jujuba* or jujube tree.

While not supplying all of the garden's water needs, a perfectly functioning well of the traditional, rain-fed Venetian type behind the apse of the church has been fitted with a pump and provides plentiful fresh water for most of the year. The seventeenth-century monastery pharmacy, now an exquisitely preserved museum, testifies to centuries of dispensing activity, many of the herbs for which would have grown in the monastery's physick garden. Beyond the low outhouses and sheds which once formed the southern boundary along the edge of the lagoon is a small garden of a more purely meditative nature. Created out of a *sacca*, or infill dumped here by the city authorities at the end of the nineteenth century, this little area with its low hillock and olive trees looks out over the vast, opalescent calm of the south lagoon.

A quite different fate has been met by another surviving convent garden behind the church of Santa Maria della Presentazione, known as the Zitelle (spinsters) because of the hospice that was once attached to it. This institution was founded in 1559 to provide training in lacemaking and

ABOVE The Bauer Palladio garden is an artful combination of past and present: old-fashioned climbing roses and *Pennisetum villosum*.
BELOW Elsewhere in the same garden, the feathery plumes of *Stipa tenuissima* in late summer lend a distinctly North American accent.
RIGHT Variation on a traditional theme in the Bauer Palladio: Isabella grapevine underplanted with catnip, iris, roses and grasses.

music to young girls from poor families in order that they might not be forced to follow other, less noble professions. The buildings that housed them are now part of the Bauer Palladio, a luxury hotel complex at the eastern end of the Giudecca, where a section of the old convent garden has been recently and tastefully redesigned for the needs of paying guests rather than the saving of souls. An ancient olive tree, an Aleppo pine and two towering yews are all that survive from former times but there are subtle hints of an older ground plan in, for example, the large rectangles of longer grass breaking up the expanse of lawn, echoing the formal, geometric layout of a monastic garden. These areas, in which myriad meadow plants are allowed to flower and set seed, are alive with butterflies and the hum of insects.

A long pergola covered with thickly growing vines and roses and lushly planted at its base with catnip, lavender, ornamental grasses, iris and aquilegia provides a shady walk towards a second garden, visible through a *claire voie* in the dividing wall. This smaller, more enclosed space at one time possessed an avenue of pollarded plane trees and these have been incorporated into a series of maze-like small rooms around a fountain bordered by loosely cut box hedges and by Annabelle and oakleaf hydrangeas. The enclosing walls are smothered in scented

roses of every shade of white and cream, palest yellow and pink-flecked apricot.

The land on which this garden is built belongs to a public institution, the IRE, one of the many old Venetian charitable organisations set up for the care and tutelage of the old, the ill and the unfortunate. The IRE also owns the land beyond the hotel garden, a huge area that was once part of the convent grounds which stretched uninterrupted to the lagoon. Although it now comprises an old people's home and a daycare centre, one important feature of the old convent garden and of island life has been retained: the vineyard. More than a hundred vines are planted here, in two main blocks, with a pergola running down the middle.

Some of the older vines have been identified as the rare local 'Dorona' variety, a white grapevine that despite being specially adapted to the soil and climate of the lagoon, had almost died out. The harvest of Merlot, Cabernet and Lambrusco Marani grapes from this and other scattered vines around Venice is taken to the island of Mazzorbo to be made into 'Rosso Gneca' (Giudecca Red), a strong, rather tannic red wine with a slightly salty aftertaste. The vineyard is looked after by volunteers, and occupants of the old people's home are encouraged by the presence of wheelchair-friendly paths, to perambulate under the pergolas. In a corner of the site, the luxuriant growth of a synergistic vegetable plot managed by another collective threatens to overwhelm its neighbour as Borlotti bean and courgette plants entwine themselves among the vine trellises and maize towers two metres in the air. This is only one of several examples on the island of a uniquely Venetian social interface, a deeply felt communitarian spirit that is rooted in a fierce attachment to the city's traditions and unique way of life, now more than ever under threat by the depredations of mass tourism which have rendered large tracts of the city centre unpleasant and uninhabitable.

This already diverse scenario is further enriched by two more institutional gardens, each remarkable in a different way but sharing the singular characteristic of being worked exclusively by women. Behind the modest premises of the Monastero della Santissima Trinità, the Poor Clare Sisters devote themselves to prayer and to the cultivation of a vineyard and olive grove. Further west, on the Rio delle Convertite, the inmates of the Giudecca women's prison tend a large organic vegetable garden and orchard in the grounds of an ex-monastery. They call their garden 'L'Orto delle Meraviglie' (the garden of wonders) and use its produce to supply the prison kitchen, selling the excess on a stall outside the prison gates once a week. Aromatic herbs are also grown, some of which are distilled for perfumers and others used directly in cosmetics made on the premises and sold to selected retailers and Venetian hotels.

It is impossible to visit today's Giudecca gardens without returning again and again in the imagination to the most famous (and biggest) one of all: the garden created from 1884 by Frederic Eden and his wife Caroline Jekyll, elder sister of Gertrude. Although the bell on its well-locked gate still bears the tantalising epithet 'Giardino

Eden', most Giudeccans refer to it as Princess Aspasia's garden, perhaps because that name has more recent and more romantic associations. The exiled morganatic widow of Alexander of Greece lived here from 1928 until her death in 1972 and the house was subsequently occupied by her daughter, the unhappy Queen Alexandra of Yugoslavia. Since the death in 2000 of its last owner, the Austrian artist Friedensreich Hundertwasser, the garden has been inaccessible, although it is still maintained by the foundation that bears his name.

In 1910 Frederic Eden published *A Garden in Venice*, a loving account of the slow transformation of an old and neglected island garden, first indicated to him by his gondolier, into a flower and fruit-filled paradise that he and his wife shared generously with bohemian and artistic visitors from all over the world for the best part of two decades. Its scented avenues, overflowing borders and secluded lawns were frequented at one time or another by Henry James, D'Annunzio, and in later years by Rilke and Cocteau, and descriptions of its charms found their way into several literary works.

LEFT A remnant of one of the original long pergolas that Frederic and Caroline Eden created here from 1884.
ABOVE Pergola and old gateway. Photograph from the original edition of *A Garden in Venice*.
RIGHT The old gateway today, recently restored. The pergola has gone but the memorial plaques to pet dogs remain.

Although an invalid from boyhood, Eden possessed enough determination and funds to see his vision realised of a place that would be artfully suggestive of natural abundance, a garden that would disprove the saying '*Venezia, tomba dei fiori*' (Venice, tomb of flowers). With 'tender regard to the genius of the place', the Edens preserved the traditional Venetian palazzo layout of squares and intersecting straight lines but rejected cut yews and clipped box as being out of character for the rural, informal atmosphere they wished to achieve. Fond memories of a Scottish garden gave them the idea of enclosing their kitchen plots with espaliered pear and apple trees, but the hot climate disagreed with this arrangement and they resorted to vine pergolas which

had the great advantage of providing lengths of shaded walkways. After much thought as to materials, it was decided to follow local tradition and fashion the pergolas from pollarded willow poles brought from the mainland. Photographs of the Eden garden show light and flexible structures receding into the far distance, underplanted with thousands of Madonna lilies.

As the years passed, the cabbages and artichokes were displaced by Dutch bulbs, followed by a cottage-garden succession of columbines, foxgloves, larkspurs, and love-in-a-mist. The vigour and size of the flowering plants they

LEFT 'Filled with water-lilies and goldfish…lemon trees in Venetian vases all around…a success.' Photograph from *A Garden in Venice*.
BELOW 'A garden would be an arid waste without water.' Eden's Vasca Grande as it appears today.
RIGHT The southern boundary of the Garden of Eden, where the Rio della Croce meets the lagoon.

introduced was at first a source of amazement to gardeners used to a less generous soil and climate, but the failures tended to be just as dramatic. Eden's account gives the impression that there was more than an element of painful trial and error in adapting to the extremes of salinity and temperature, the violence of the lagoon storms and, not least, the unpredictability of the workforce.

To their delight, the Edens found that most roses flourished happily in their garden so they planted and propagated hundreds for, as Frederic wrote, '…the joy of a garden lies, more or less, in its wealth; one loves to see things grow as if they liked it'. Further inspiration for this 'English' garden came from Moorish Spain where the Edens had admired the use of water in the Generalife in Granada. The consequent drilling of an artesian well to feed a large tank led to many illuminating and costly adventures, entertainingly documented by Eden in his

book. This tank, latterly used as a swimming pool, survives, now bereft of its surrounding lemon trees in pots. After land reclamation by the city authorities extended the south shore of the island, the Edens bought an extra two acres of building rubble and mud and proceeded to convert it into a vineyard. They were almost self-sufficient but the addition of a small dairy herd necessitated the buying of pastureland further afield: hay for the cows' fodder was ferried from the island of Sant'Erasmo in the northern lagoon, to this day the market garden of Venice.

The stories that gardens tell are soon obscured. A few years of neglect brings pergolas crashing down, disfigures statuary and dislodges pavements. The Eden Garden has not quite been lost but it is difficult to imagine how its old-world splendour could ever be recreated. Rumours abound, but the gate to the little bridge that crosses Rio della Croce remains tight shut.

PALAZZO CAPPELLO MALIPIERO BARNABÒ

FEW GARDEN LOVERS GAZING OUT FROM a boat at the procession of imposing palazzi along the Grand Canal will have failed to notice the explosion of flowers, foliage and statuary that suddenly bursts out between two high buildings on a bend of the city's main waterway. Clambering over a low marble balustrade which seems only with difficulty to restrain the vegetable growth within, pink roses seethe like a tide towards the water while beyond, the deeper pinks of oleanders are massed in brilliant light before the dark boughs of an old thuja. It is as if another Venice were breaking through the magnificently ornate façade of coloured marble and stucco, a Venice whose existence we had suspected but never actually glimpsed, hidden as it almost always is behind high brick walls. As the boat swings over towards Ca' Rezzonico, the garden, like a mirage, disappears from sight, leaving only an impression of airiness, light and perfume that soon dissipates as the landing stage is approached to an accompanying roar from the engine, puffs of diesel smoke and the bustle of disembarking passengers.

The garden of Palazzo Cappello Malipiero Barnabò is notable for several reasons, not least because of its site. Since Venice's inception, the buildings lining its biggest canal, the 'Canalazzo' as it was popularly known, had provided warehouses as well as residences for the richer merchants and their families. With the passing of the centuries, as members of the nobility competed to raise their profile and prestige, the palazzi grew grander and more magnificent and all available space along the canal

was built upon. The open area within a palazzo, vital for the collection of rainwater, was sited well back from the canal, on the other side of the *androne* or entrance hall with its water door, and consisted of a paved courtyard with one or, if space permitted, several well-heads. Rainwater flowing off the roofs and falling on the ground was directed into a series of underground conduits that in turn led to a tank with a filtering system consisting of graded sand. The water then passed into a central shaft lined with special porous bricks, from which it could be raised to the surface in a bucket. The system took advantage of Venice's almost impervious substratum of clay and was an ingenious way of getting round the otherwise intractable problem of providing fresh drinking water. Unsurprisingly, well-heads came to be invested with great symbolic importance, and the Istrian stone from which they were made was often richly decorated with sculptural relief. Sometimes, there were larger spaces

LEFT The symmetry underlying the garden's profusion of blooms is best appreciated in this view from above.
RIGHT A miniature rose adds its airy grace to the prickly leaves of acanthus on this five-hundred-year-old well-head.

beyond the well area, so that the courtyard became an anteroom to a garden in the sense of a space dedicated to the growing of plants for ornamental and practical use. But in this case the empty space that made the creation of a garden on the Grand Canal possible resulted from the demolition of an adjoining building.

A well-head in the centre of the garden commemorates the marriage, on 22 April 1597, of Elisabetta Cappello to Catterino Malipiero. Around this time a small neighbouring house with a walled vegetable plot was incorporated into the Cappello-Malipiero property. Major adjustments were made to the building around 1622 in order to create two apartments with separate entrances, one each from the canal and one each from the adjacent *campo*. The palazzo, which still bears faint traces of the Venetian–Byzantine style, therefore has an unusual layout, with two L-shaped entrance halls running beneath the *piano nobile*, or main floor, only one of which, however, leads to the garden.

The famous theatre of San Samuele, where the playwright Carlo Goldoni made his debut, opened in 1665 just a few streets away, and in the eighteenth century the area was much frequented by theatregoers and players. Giacomo Casanova, whose parents were both actors with travelling companies, was born in a house nearby and, as an adolescent, was a frequent visitor at Palazzo Malipiero, having befriended the old senator Alvise Malipiero, a bachelor who 'lived a beatific life in his palazzo, eating good meals and hosting a select society of gentlewomen every evening'. It was here that Casanova first met Teresa Imer, the future theatre impresario and mother of his daughter Sophie, when they were both little more than children.

It was not until the Barnabò family took possession of the palazzo in 1890 that the garden began to be organised into something approaching its present layout. By a stroke of good luck, their purchase coincided with the demolition of Palazzo Lion Cavazza in the parish of Santa Lucia, to make way for the railway station. During the seventeenth century Count Girolamo Cavazza had displayed his renowned collections of sculptures, paintings and furniture in a museum on the ground floor of his palazzo. It is believed that the sculpture of Neptune which forms the centrepiece of the Barnabò garden was salvaged from this site, since a description of an identical statue is given in Giustiniano Martinioni's additions to Francesco Sansovino's *Venetia, città nobilissima et singolare*, an extraordinarily detailed chronicle of the city written in 1583 and amplified in 1663.

The garden is approached through the lofty *androne* just inside the main door of the palazzo from the street, and is

The first indication of a garden existing on the site is given in an engraving dating from 1828–29 by Dionisio Moretti, which shows a high brick wall with a row of tall trees growing behind it. During this period, the Malipiero family having become extinct, the palazzo was rented out to Leopoldo Cicognara (1767–1834), a scholar and art historian who was president of the Accademia di Belle Arti from 1808. He undertook a complete restoration of the palazzo, filling it with antiquities and embellishing it with frescoes, and it is tempting to think that his artistic and antiquarian interests may have led him to intervene in the garden also.

LEFT The marble balustrade allows extra visibility, inviting the gaze of the passer-by on the Grand Canal.
ABOVE From the penumbra of the *androne*, the first glimpse of the garden is designed to enthrall.
RIGHT A putto strains to hold a fish-like serpent in the pond while behind, Neptune reinforces the water theme.

hallway. Past the entrance and across the courtyard is an open wrought-iron gate that interrupts a low wall running across the line of sight. Tussling figures grapple with each other atop rusticated plinths at either side of this opening where stone steps lead up to the garden proper. Inscriptions identify the warring figures as Jupiter and Ganymede on the left and Hercules and Antaeus on the right. The courtyard, paved in the familiar trachyte of Venice's streets, has three well-heads which were probably moved to one side, after the arrival of mains

LEFT Bonazza's sculpture of Autumn cuts a dashing figure, a quiver full of arrows slung over his shoulder.
BELOW A weathered Flora holds a bunch of flowers, accompanied by a fawn-like creature at her feet.
RIGHT The muted pinks and whites of roses, hibiscus and Japanese anemones are a perfect accompaniment to the gleam of white stone.

immediately visible as a well of light at the further end. A letter 'B' in wrought-iron curlicues above the arched entrance to the courtyard leaves no doubt as to its ownership. The excitement of approaching a garden that only reveals itself by stages is deliberately enhanced by a series of framing devices that both invite and delay exploration of the space beyond. Already the creamy, sinuous forms of sculptures can be glimpsed in greenish light and the scent of fresh foliage reaches down the

water in the nineteenth century, in order to clear a central axis. Neptune, his legs entwined with a sea monster, is contained in a niche within a specially built nymphaeum standing against the far wall, in which two sets of twin columns support small statues of reclining river gods. In a central space in front of this, bordered by a flourish of low box hedges, an elegantly shaped pond lies flush with the white gravel, bursting with water lilies.

The garden's L-shape now becomes apparent, since the pond lies at the intersection of the garden's two axes. To the right, stretching down to the stone balustrade overlooking the Grand Canal are two sets of two long rectangular beds containing lawns within which are planted a variety of floribunda, hybrid tea and standard roses in various shades of pink. The grey-green foliage of pinks is sometimes used as a narrow border around their roots. Early in the year, irises and mimosa expand the colour palette until overtaken by an eruption of perfume and bloom from the pittosporum and *Trachelospermum jasminoides* that line the walls on either side. Oleander, hibiscus and, later, the cool pink of hydrangeas dominate in summer while the roses recover enough for a second flowering at the beginning of autumn, accompanied by a flush of white Japanese anemones.

The rounded, bushy forms of flowering shrubs that everywhere soften the underlying geometric structure, the rose-covered bower and the two female statues looking out, cornucopia in hand, over the canal, lend the garden

a graceful, feminine appearance. Even the four statues in creamy white Vicenza stone by Antonio Bonazza (1698–1763) of four rustic male types, do little to dispel this impression. Spaced in the corners of the central area around the pool, these allegories of the Four Seasons are closely observed and jauntily characterised. Their vigorous quality brings the breath of the countryside into this urban plot, yet their placing among sprays of soft pink

roses and perfumed jasmine creates a note of wistful nostalgia. Bonazza was from a prolific Paduan family of sculptors and is best known for the sixteen life-size genre sculptures in the garden of Villa Widmann at Bagnoli di Sopra, near Padua.

The latest restoration of house and garden took place in 1951 when the present layout was defined, an imaginative and pleasing arrangement that has a vaguely eighteenth-century air. For the last twenty-five years, under the loving eye of Countess Anna Barnabò, it has been gardened with the perseverance necessary for a garden on the edge of the restless tides.

LEFT A mass of pink and white roses forms a thorny but ineffective barrier to the briny canal water.
ABOVE The forecourt with its monumental sculptures. Beyond, Summer pauses, startled, in the act of playing a flute.

PALAZZO SORANZO CAPPELLO

THE AIR OF QUIET DISCOURAGEMENT noted by the narrator of Henry James's 1888 novella *The Aspern Papers* no longer lingers around Palazzo Soranzo Cappello. Overlooking a quiet canal in the *sestiere* of Santa Croce, the seventeenth-century palazzo with its large garden was the house that James 'had more or less in mind' in his description of the home of two of the most haunting characters in his fiction: the enigmatic Misses Bordereau. A long and thorough restoration has replaced the building's peeling grey stucco with well appointed pink, and a modest brass plaque has been fitted by the door to indicate that the premises are now the headquarters of the Soprintendenza per i Beni Architettonici e per il Paesaggio del Veneto Orientale. If ever there was an occasion to showcase the work of the governmental organisation responsible for architectural and landscape heritage, this is it.

Palazzo Soranzo Cappello had long languished in a state of abandonment until, in 1989, it was bought by the state by means of the right of pre-emption and the long job of restoration got underway, lasting until 2003. Its sizeable garden was an impenetrable thicket of bay laurel, elder, paper mulberry and privet, while swathes of pungent wild garlic and cuckoo pint covered every last inch of ground not already smothered by ivy. A thick canopy of large deciduous trees shaded the garden in summer and had wrought havoc with the once stuccoed high brick wall that snaked unsteadily around the garden's perimeter. But all that is a thing of the past. After polite enquiry at the porter's lodge has elicited an affirmative nod, one is left to one's own devices to pass through the atrium to the double doors at the far end, push down on the brass handle and discover a very special garden.

The newly restored forms of twelve Roman emperors line the grassy courtyard; Julius Caesar stands in a central position on the left, while the main niche on the right is occupied by a statue of Augustus, whose rule heralded the so-called golden age of Roman art and literature. These lofty references to ancient history are mitigated by the homely presence of two *Diospyros kaki* trees, much beloved of Venetians for their glossy green foliage and for the sweet, fleshy persimmons that on foggy November days will glow like lanterns on their bare and blackened branches. At its far end, the courtyard is enclosed by a low wall topped by a wrought-iron fence, a time-honoured

LEFT Wrought-iron gates and groups of struggling figures mark the separation between forecourt and garden.
RIGHT The view down the garden towards the loggia from the courtyard of the Caesars.

method of separating such outer rooms from the garden proper. It acts as visual filter, creating both a feeling of suspense and a degree of awareness of what lies on the other side. Two pillars frame the gated opening in this wall, supporting finely sculpted pairs of struggling nudes that have been attributed to Orazio Marinali (1643–1720). The subject matter has been variously identified as the Rape of the Sabines or, more recently, the Labours of Hercules.

Beyond the wall, the trachyte paving gives way to a gravel path that leads straight along the central axis to the bottom of the garden, where the Roman theme is echoed by a loggia. The three remaining sculptures on its tympanum, representing allegorical figures of virtues, may have been part of a series that included the three similar sculptures placed on the corners of the garden wall; Abundance, Merit, Fame, Concord, Strength and Trust continue to impart their weathered message of

exhortation. The areas just outside the courtyard and in front of the loggia are slightly more formal in arrangement, as if the nearby architecture played a greater role in defining them. Terracotta pots with citrus trees and other tender species grace the garden side of the courtyard with their civilising and ornamental presence. The loggia built against the garden's rear wall, its eight columns forming a shallow, covered space, is purely an architectural conceit but lends that certain air of classical distinction that was a fashionable means in the Baroque period for Venetian noble families to express their political and social ascendancy. At the turn of the seventeenth and eighteenth centuries, Lorenzo Soranzo's career culminated in ambassadorial appointments to England and Constantinople and it may be to this period that the garden owes its creation. Certainly it was already famous enough to be included in the series of woodcuts of the wonders of Venice published in 1709 by the cartographer monk Vincenzo Coronelli and entitled *Singolarità di Venezia*. But it was only at the turn of the nineteenth and twentieth centuries, when it was already in a state of some neglect, that the garden of Palazzo Soranzo Cappello garnered its most famous literary associations.

It is to this period of its history that the garden's recent restoration makes reference. Inspiration was taken both from James's crepuscular fable of turn-of-the-century Venice and from the detailed notes made by Gabriele D'Annunzio for the setting of his novel *Il fuoco* (translated into English as *The Flame of Life*), published in 1900. The decision to leave in place many of the large trees that had

grown unchecked in the intervening years was prompted partly by the wish to screen off the surrounding buildings, but partly also in deference to what James's hero describes as the garden's 'weeds and its wild rich tangle, its sweet characteristic Venetian shabbiness'. In a sort of homage to the years in which the garden was left to its own devices, a substantial area in the centre is devoted to the woodland plants that had naturalised here, together with some introductions for the sake of variety. Violets, periwinkle, hellebores and aquilegia contribute their flowers before the tree canopy throws them into the deep shade of the summer months. The intention has been to hint at past forms rather than reinstate them, and to delineate a possible, but not definitive future arrangement, in which the central axis will be progressively cleared and the sides of the garden more filled out. As James's hero rightly observed, throwing

LEFT The massive forms of the emperors lend gravitas to this area of the garden, carpeted with spring flowers.
BELOW A swathe of *Iris japonica* bordering the lawns keeps the 'wild' woodland in its place.

Veduta dal Giardino.

open a shutter on the first floor, this 'garden in the middle of the sea', as he put it, has 'great capabilities'.

To D'Annunzio is owed the rebuilding of the pergolas running along the boundary walls on either side, planted with white and pink rambling roses such as 'Adelaide d'Orleans' and 'Super Dorothy' (the latter replacing the popular early twentieth-century 'Dorothy Perkins') as well as *Jasminum officinale*:

LEFT Coronelli's engraving shows squares of *broderie* parterre divided by a central path lined with sculptures.
BELOW A vine pergola running across the side garden intersects with the central axis of mown grass.
RIGHT *Jasminum officinale* is paired with Concord and Muscadelle grapevines, ensuring deep shade as summer advances.

In the garden, the guests had dispersed along the walks and under the vine-trellises. The night air was damp and lukewarm; delicate eyelids could feel it on their lashes like the approach of a warm, mobile mouth. The hidden stars of the Jessamine shrubs yielded their acute perfume in the shadow; the odour of the fruits too was as strong and even heavier than in the island gardens. A vivid fertilizing power emanated from that small space of cultivated earth that was enclosed like an exiled thing by its girdle of water, becoming all the more intense from its banishment, like the soul of the exile.

The nocturnal sensuality of D'Annunzio's description is evoked by an underplanting of irises, white lilies and foxgloves. The heroine of *Il fuoco*, Foscarina, is a thinly-disguised version of the great actress Eleonora Duse with whom the writer had a long and tempestuous affair. The wild, impulsive nature of their relationship is symbolised by the lovers' preference for entering the garden by way of the abandoned and overgrown plot of neighbouring Palazzo Gradenigo, through a hole in the wall of Foscarina's making. Today, a glance from the canalside through the wrought-iron grilles shows that the much-reduced garden of the latter is now a well-cared for oasis of green. Once, however, this truly enormous park stretched along the Grand Canal almost as far as the present-day Papadopoli gardens and was famous in the eighteenth century for its lavish outdoor parties and banquets as well as for its wide avenues for carriages and horse riding. From 1920, it disappeared under new housing for railway workers.

The side garden, entered both from the main garden and directly from the *fondamenta* or canalside, lies on the palazzo's left flank and its original designation as a *brolo*, or orchard, has been reinstated. Old varieties of Maraschino cherry, pear and pomegranate have been planted in a poppy and cornflower-filled meadow that recalls a small country orchard. The two pergolas constructed in the traditional Venetian manner with sweet chestnut poles are rustic in appearance, but the materials used are in fact wholly authentic. The result is ethereal but not frail, sturdy but not everlasting and, like the poles of robinia used as mooring posts in the canals, sooner or later they will have

to be replaced. The planting of these pergolas with grapevines, under which run double rows of lilies, interspersed with iris, Jacob's ladder and aquilegia, deliberately echoes the descriptions of Frederic Eden's long pergolas in his garden on the Giudecca (see page 36). Although such pergolas had been a feature of the Venetian city garden long before Eden copied them, it took an Englishman's love of flowers to modify the tradition by adding blooms in glorious profusion.

Everywhere in this garden a balance has been struck between respect for tradition and the intelligent use of modern techniques. Whereas the Venetian city garden layout never strayed far from a pergola running straight down the central axis of the garden, this has been avoided

in both the main and the orchard gardens in favour of opening up the central vistas. The memory of former structures is retained, however, by cutting the grass at different heights, as if the past had left its shadow imprinted on the ground.

This has the added advantage of allowing the rich mélange of wild flowers in the lawns to set seed, ensuring their survival the following year. In the courtyard of the Roman emperors this is particularly important since its four small lawns are crammed with spring-flowering bulbs. A helpful notice records their names. They include *Anemone blanda*, *Fritillaria meleagris*, *Iris reticulata*, crocus, grape hyacinth, and two different varieties of *Narcissus triandrus*, 'Thalia' and 'Hawera'. There is also *Scilla siberica*, but no mention is made of *Hyacinthoides non-scripta*, the native British bluebell that Countess Marina Emo reports as filling the little courtyard with their elusive scent in early spring (see Villa Emo, page 118). This can

only mean that they were already here, so the question arises as to who might have planted them.

The plot of *The Aspern Papers*, in which a literary biographer becomes obsessed with gaining possession of a hoard of love letters written by his favourite (and long dead) poet to his mistress, was based on the real-life story of Claire Clairmont, one of Byron's mistresses, who lived on in Florence until her death in 1879. By transposing the tale to Venice, James conceded himself more artistic licence, setting his story against the backdrop of the decaying city and selecting models for his characters from among his many expatriate friends there. One such was the American-born writer Julia Constance Fletcher (1858–1938) who lived in Palazzo Soranzo Cappello with her mother and her stepfather, the American painter Eugene Benson.

Fletcher was something of a prodigy, publishing a best-selling novel at the age of eighteen, under the pseudonym

she would use for the rest of her life, George Fleming. A year later, in 1877, she published a second novel, *Mirage*, basing one of her characters on Oscar Wilde, whom she had met in Rome some months earlier. In return, Wilde, who was still an undergraduate at Oxford, dedicated his poem *Ravenna* to her. By an odd coincidence, the portentous nature of which cannot fail to have struck Henry James, Fletcher was rumoured to have had an ill-fated romantic liaison in her youth with Lord Byron's grandson, Ralph King-Milbanke, 2nd Earl of Lovelace. Like Claire Clairmont, she too never subsequently married. Pursuing a career as a journalist, novelist and playwright, she moved increasingly between London and Venice, but eventually returned permanently to Palazzo Soranzo Cappello to care for her invalid parents. In 1911 she met Gertrude Stein and Alice B. Toklas at Mabel Dodge's villa in Tuscany. Stein wrote a prose portrait of her that was

published in *Geography and Plays* in 1922. The portrait includes suggestions of flowers, light, bells, statues, and ends with the ominous words, 'the shadow which is larger is not flickering', perhaps an allusion to her subject's failing creative powers.

Fletcher/Fleming's novels are full of descriptions of flowers, both wild and cultivated. *Mirage* is set in Palestine and Syria, but Palazzo Soranzo Cappello does not seem far away:

> … They pushed open the creaking gate and passed from out the noisy street into an old and silent garden – an up-springing wilderness of rose-bushes and oranges, with here and there a mossy peach-tree thrusting a branch of pale pink blossoms across the narrow path.

Might those bluebells have been planted by Julia Constance Fletcher?

LEFT The central path, until recently obliterated by undergrowth, has been reinstated, opening up the garden's main vista.
ABOVE Trust cradling a galleon in her left arm retains her place on top of the wall at the far end of the garden.
RIGHT Like a suite of rooms in a Venetian palazzo, one garden space gives onto another by way of a door.

FONDAZIONE QUERINI STAMPALIA

THE SMALLEST GARDEN BY FAR IN THE present volume is one that, in inverse proportion to its scale, repays long contemplation. It is first sighted from the *campiello* or little square opposite the sixteenth-century palazzo that until 1869 was the home of the patrician Querini Stampalia family. By the terms of the will of its last descendant, Count Giovanni Querini Stampalia, the house and its contents were transformed into a public library and museum, with the stipulation that the reading room should remain open at those times when other libraries in the city were normally closed. Men and women of learning would thus, reasoned the scholarly and childless count, have a place to meet in the comfort of a reading room that would be furnished with heaters and carpets to combat the damp chill of winter evenings.

Today his wishes continue to be abundantly fulfilled, benefiting the hundreds of readers who use the library on the first floor, and the thousands of visitors to the museum, bookshop, exhibitions of contemporary art, conferences, seminars, film screenings and concerts

LEFT Staggered cast concrete walls frame a view of the pond inset within a pond from the café area.

ABOVE Sunlight hits the back wall of the Scarpa garden, and is reflected off the highly polished ceiling of Venetian plaster.

organised by the foundation that bears his name. His dream for the family palazzo has perhaps exceeded his expectations, but for the dank, enclosed courtyard behind it, he evidently had none. Writing to his factor in 1866, Count Giovanni said he was reluctant to spend much in the way of plants for the garden since his aim was simply to cover the walls, and for that purpose the Japanese laurel already planted by the gardener would do, if, that is, they did not die first. What he could not have foreseen, as he desultorily ordered a few more ill-fated aromatic plants to add to that place of no account, was that it would one day become one of the most inspirational gardens in the city and a landmark in twentieth-century architecture.

The decision to commission the Venetian-born Carlo Scarpa (1906–78) to remodel the ground floor of the historic building, and with it the outdoor space at the back, was taken by the foundation's director Manlio Dazzi in

1950. Scarpa was building a reputation as a brilliant and innovative designer-architect who had made something of a specialism out of remodelling exhibition and teaching spaces within pre-existing buildings. His first ideas for the garden of the Querini Stampalia included a labyrinth with a fountain in its midst, but this was set aside as other projects took precedence during the decade, notably the restoration and reworking of Palazzo Abatellis in Palermo and the Museum of Castelvecchio in Verona, both ancient complexes with centuries-old accretions of interventions in various architectural styles.

When Luigi Mazzariol took over as the new director of the foundation, the project to transform the dilapidated and under-used ground floor and garden of the palazzo was relaunched and building work finally began in 1961, to be completed in 1963. Scarpa's task involved redesigning the space directly inside the *porte ad acqua* or water doors

giving onto the canal, and reclaiming the dark and damp interiors which were prone to flooding at high tide. The 17 × 8 metre courtyard at the back of the palazzo, overlooked by the library, backing onto a high brick wall and crowded with temporary storerooms, was to be incorporated into the redesign as a low-maintenance garden. Taking account of the traditional Venetian handling of such ground-floor spaces, in which a central atrium opening directly from the canal leads into an outdoor courtyard beyond, and then the garden proper, Scarpa went further and conceived the whole area as a unitary space in which there is no interruption in the view from the palazzo's façade to the wall at the rear of the garden. The continuity from one space to the next is enhanced by means of wrought-iron gates in a simple, modern design across the two arched water entrances and by glass doors inserted at either end of the atrium. Thus, from the *campiello* across the canal, the white sculptural elements of the garden seem to float mirage-like over the green, while canal traffic may be seen from the garden, gliding by outside the front of the building. A steel and timber footbridge spans the canal and leads directly into the building by a door (once a window) flanking the water gates.

Since *acqua alta* or high tides are increasingly a fact of life in the city, Scarpa took a Venetian view of it as a resource rather than a constraint; he saw water as an element that could be allowed to enter the building, as indeed it always had, but in a controlled way that would permit him to exploit it for its symbolism and its decorative effect. Canal water slops over and through the wrought-iron gates into a pit with slabs of stone leading up to ground-floor level. As the tide comes and goes, so the steps emerge and are submerged. If the water level rises beyond the steps, it is directed into channels that run round the perimeter of the front atrium space and if any higher, it fills the shallow reliefs cut into the centre of the floor. Finally, when there is a particularly high tide, part of the atrium becomes flooded, but this is an event that is factored into the design and indeed the building acquires an added, ethereal beauty from its temporary presence.

LEFT The shimmering nature of water is captured in this frieze of mosaic tesserae designed by artist Mario De Luigi.
ABOVE The water gates at the entrance let in light, air and, crucially, water which can rise above the low parapet.

The garden may be approached either from a side corridor or from the sala Luzzatti, a conference space that occupies the former *portego* (as the large space running below the Venetian palazzo and connecting the canal with dry land was called). Light flickers in from the canal end, in constantly moving patterns made by the reflections of sunlight on water, while the raised lawn at the other end tinges with a greenish hue the more subdued light entering from the garden. The floor, a geometrical arrangement of aggregate concrete divided by bands of Istrian stone, continues through and beyond the glass doors into the garden where four columns from the original building, now devoid of any structural role, create a sort of portico for the little courtyard. Here too, Scarpa followed Venetian type, with a paved area and steps up to the garden, raised in order to protect plants from the tides. The sound of water is what we notice first: no longer the brackish, milky swill of the canal but a shimmering, crystalline presence flowing cleanly along a narrow channel encased in the low concrete

retaining wall that runs perpendicularly across almost
the entire breadth of the garden.

The water originates from two tiny spouts that direct
it into a small grey-streaked marble tray with maze-like
compartments of subtly different depths, from where it
must find its way, as in a child's game, to the exit. It is, in
its way, a miniature fountain, but its unique form raises
questions about movement, stillness, the action of running
water. Lily pads cover the entire surface of the narrow
channel that catches this water, their round forms and
glinting surfaces a perfect foil to the monotone linearity
of the cast concrete wall. As it reaches its destination at
the far end, the water encounters an obstacle in the form

RIGHT Water flows inconspicuously to the side of the lion into
a collecting tank behind, planted with papyrus.
BELOW The three elements of Italian garden design: stone, water
and evergreen in a twentieth-century reworking.

of a plinth on which an antique stone lion crouches, momentarily distracted from gnawing a human head held between its paws. It is a humorous allusion to the centuries-old symbol of Venice's might, but beautifully placed just at the point where the low wall turns a right angle, marking the juncture between the lower and upper levels of the garden. Behind the lion, papyrus stems jut out at angles from the water, their fan-like leaves evoking Egypt and the invention of paper – somewhat aptly given the building's function as a library. As the water trickles out of an adjustable steel spout into a carved travertine slab below, the play of associations on a Venetian theme continues as it is then carried away in a trough that runs beneath a large marble well-head. The connection having been made between water and well, this brings to mind the ingenuity of the city's first inhabitants in ensuring a supply of fresh water. 'The city in water that had no water', as it was once described, relied wholly on rainwater collected in underground cisterns where it was filtered by layers of sand and sealed with clay. Rendered obsolete by the arrival of the aqueduct in 1884, the public wells still visible in most Venetian *campi* are often elaborately decorated and some are of great antiquity. Here, Scarpa introduces a playful element by raising the redundant well-head's immensely heavy round form on small round plinths, so that it seems to float, disconnected from its support. Its hollow centre is filled with plants, in a further allusion to its former function as a container for the fount of all life.

'I'm a Byzantine at heart,' Scarpa once remarked, 'A European sailing towards the Orient.' He made his first visit to Japan in the 1950s and was profoundly influenced by Japanese design. Here it is perhaps discernible in the absolute simplicity and quietude of a garden that is pared down to its essentials, in which there is nothing in excess and no compulsion to fill empty space. The measured shapes and subtle differences of tone of the various evergreens combine to create an atmosphere of meditative restraint. Ivy and *Ficus pumila* cover the high brick wall bordering the garden at the rear, while the lawn at its base is empty, interrupted only by L-shaped stepping stones set into the ground. Elsewhere, periwinkle is used to create

uniform areas of glossy dark green, and the heart-shaped leaves of sweet violet colonise the edges of the lawn, but the plant elements are few and understated. A Japanese flowering cherry, a Judas tree and a *Magnolia soulangeana* share the lawn space, taking turns to produce their pink and purplish blossoms in the spring. They are succeeded by a pomegranate, whose compact habit, dark coral flowers and edible fruit make it a popular choice for the restricted space of Venetian gardens.

The garden invites us, by steps and stopping places at various levels, to walk around it, to notice how we place a foot, how we shift our weight, pause or change direction, moving with hand and eye and foot. Low containing walls provide seating at different heights, giving different views of the garden and allowing us to hear the different tonalities of the water sounds. Wherever the eye falls there is some detail to fascinate it, some piece of exquisite craftsmanship that articulates a corner or a join, or some minutely planned embellishment of, and commentary upon, two juxtaposed materials. These are few and used with a rigorous honesty, enhancing each other's structural or decorative qualities. Each, from the most humble to the most precious, is accorded its own particular status,

RIGHT The results of Scarpa's almost obsessive belief in craftsmanship continue to astonish.

whether brutalist cast concrete or the shimmering transparencies of Murano glass tesserae. To Venice's famously off-square buildings, Scarpa has responded in kind. After a while it becomes clear that any lines we might have taken for granted as straight are nothing of the sort; they are all subtly but determinedly non-parallel.

At the far end of the garden, a young child is bent over the shallow pond that encloses another raised pond in copper, prodding leaves with a twig, examining the millions of possibilities of action and reaction of the elements of which she is the temporary master. The sun has dropped

behind the high surrounding buildings, leaving the garden in shadow like the bottom of a well. Her parents want to go home but she can't leave, not just yet. She is immersed, as Scarpa wished her to be, in that insightful reverie which is the precondition for true knowledge.

BELOW LEFT From Japan Scarpa learned that space is something experienced rather than measurable.
BELOW RIGHT Every aspect has been studied down to the last detail, yet for the viewer, the feeling of discovery remains.
RIGHT Manipulation of water levels in the copper-lined pool produces subtle effects.

BRENTA

CANAL

VILLA PISANI

STRA

A SHAFT OF TEPID WINTER LIGHT REACHES in through the high windows of a long room. There is a living, breathing presence of massed foliage, glossy, robust and studded all over with glowing orange and yellow fruits. A gardener is in attendance. Although it is lunchtime on a Sunday, the cosseted occupants of a hundred antique terracotta vases cannot be allowed to wait for their sprinkling of water and their ration of fertilizer. Suddenly it is obvious why these beautiful, generous plants that respond to careful cultivation by fruiting and flowering all year long, have always aroused such passion. In a few months they will return to their plinths in the nearby *vaseria*, there to grace with their exquisite perfume the garden within the garden of Villa Pisani. The traces of an exceptional chapter in horticultural history are everywhere apparent: from the lovingly restored *tepidarium* for overwintering the plants to the various sheds for repairing the pots and housing the ingeniously designed apparatus used to lift and move them. In the villas of Northern Italy, citrus growing started as a fashion and, as the handwritten sales receipts on display show, grew during the eighteenth and nineteenth centuries into a full-scale industry. At one point, between 15,000 and 20,000 lemons were grown here annually, with income also from grapefruit, mandarins, chinotti, bergamot and citrons, not to mention the 'odorosissimi naranzi' as the oranges were termed.

Not that the owners of this villa were in any need of spare cash. Among the enormous fortunes amassed by the merchants of Venice, few could compare with that of the Pisani family of Santo Stefano. They had branched out into banking and property, accumulating unprecedented wealth which enabled them finally to have their name inscribed in the *Libro d'Oro*, the register of the Venetian nobility. By the early eighteenth century several members of the family had attained high office in the state, others had begun to dedicate themselves to culture and learning and, while the Republic entered its last century of decline, the Pisani contributed by providing a final flourish of pomp and extravagance. The usual Venetian method for showcasing a family's power and influence was to build a palazzo on the Grand Canal, but the brothers Alvise and Almorò Pisani opted for another solution. In 1718 they commissioned Girolamo Frigimelica Roberti to plan a new country villa for them on the fashionable banks of the Brenta Canal. The erudite and aristocratic Frigimelica, who considered himself more of a poet and librettist than an architect, had already designed a new wing for their palazzo in Venice. While Alvise continued to pursue his

LEFT The landing stage for Villa Pisani from the Brenta Canal, complete with Venetian striped mooring posts and *bricole*.
RIGHT Allegorical figures in the sheltered *vaseria*, where the citrus trees are set out in spring and summer.

political ambitions, eventually becoming the 114th doge in 1735, Almorò curated his art and coin collections, added to his library and oversaw the grandiose project.

In common with many Venetian noble families, the Pisani were already in the habit of escaping the sultry summer climate of Venice by removing to their villa on the mainland. The pleasant and picturesque area was within easy reach of Venice and the presence of everyone who mattered made it possible to continue, indeed to enhance, one's social life. The journey was made by *burchiello*, a specially built cabined vessel powered by sail or, in the absence of wind, by oar, as far as Fusina on the edge of the lagoon, then hitched to a horse and dragged to its destination up the Naviglio del Brenta.

On a bend in the river by the village of Stra, work began to demolish the existing Pisani villa and to lay out the park which would surround the new house. Frigimelica had completed his designs by 1719, but only the garden and some of the secondary constructions were ever built as he intended. A second, younger architect, Francesco Maria Preti, was later engaged to remodel

Frigimelica's plans and the villa, with its 114 rooms, was not properly begun until 1735, perhaps under the impetus of Alvise's recent elevation to doge. Alvise's previous political career had taken him as ambassador to the courts of France, Austria and Spain, so he was well acquainted with the ways and fashions of European royalty. At Stra, at long last, he had a chance to indulge his princely leanings.

The park designed by Le Nôtre in 1661 at the Palace of Versailles was the highpoint of the French formal garden style. Alvise, who is likely to have been taken on tours around its broad gravel avenues to admire its carefully planned vistas, the geometry of its *tapis vert*, its canals (especially the Grand Canal and *Petite Venise*) and *pièces d'eau*, its fountains, *parterres*, the variety and quantity of its statuary and then the mouth-watering visions in its *orangerie*, may well also have taken part in the numerous *fêtes galantes* with which Louis XIV liked to amuse his

BELOW Frigimelica's intricate labyrinth is still a source of merriment – and sometimes anguish – for today's visitors.
RIGHT The labyrinth tower is manned by a weary guard whose job it is to direct the disoriented out.

aristocratic guests. In exporting such ideas to the Veneto, of course, certain concessions had to be made, for despite all his Byzantine splendour, a Venetian doge was not the Sun King and the homely charms of Stra could never rival the stupefying grandeur of Versailles. Nonetheless the Villa Pisani garden was a radical departure from the traditional model of the villa Veneto, which had always been conceived as having, first and foremost, an agrarian function.

The immediate compulsion of the visitor on entering the villa's twin courtyards is to pass out through the central rear door where he will find himself aligned with the long ribbon of water that forms the main axis of the garden. At the far end, Frigimelica's magnificent pavilion, an eclectic mix of Renaissance and Baroque styles, is reflected, mirror-like in its still waters. It is an enchanting view and has achieved almost iconic status, but it is in fact a modern conceit, the concrete *peschiera* or fish pond having been built in 1911 by the Hydraulic Engineering Department of Padua University in order to test ships' models. Originally this vast green space was covered in a *broderie* parterre, on either side of which groves of trees were planted, with gravel paths running through them to create two main north-south vistas.

Most of the features that form the thirty-hectare pleasure garden are to the east of this central section of the park and were apparently among the first things completed: it would have made perfect sense to have a few years' growth on the hornbeam hedges of the labyrinth, for example, before letting one's friends loose in it. The labyrinth was just one of the many amusements planned to dazzle and delight guests at the villa. It is formed of nine broken concentric rings, replanted in box in the twentieth century, and is notorious for its difficulty. The Italian writer Gabriele D'Annunzio set a memorable scene of his autobiographical novel *Il fuoco* here, in which the heroine becomes hopelessly lost. In the centre is a tower with an ornate double helix stairway running round the outside, giving access to a viewing gallery. From here, it is possible to see the whole design and to direct people towards the tower or towards the exit, though the problem remains for the last man out. Fittingly, a statue of Minerva, the Roman goddess of wisdom stands on top. Unlike the labyrinth at Valsanzibio which has a metaphorical significance, the labyrinth at Villa Pisani is perhaps no more than a light-hearted game, and it is the only part of the garden where the visitor is allowed to feel anything approaching confusion.

The meticulously planned perspectival views and grand vistas that criss-cross the park are now partially obscured by trees but the rigid geometry of straight, intersecting paths and pergolas still leads us inexorably to explore the tantalising sights at their far end. Strategically placed wrought-iron gates and windows perforating the boundary wall allow the eye to rove beyond the park into the surrounding countryside, at the same time permitting curious outsiders to be awed by the ordered visions within. That the garden and its contents be visible from the outside appears to have been a preoccupation from the very beginning, for in 1724, before building on the villa was even underway, two rusticated gateways with windows on either side were built to flank the future villa's façade and to provide a frame for the two marble sculptural groups by Antonio Bonazza within the garden wall.

The inclusion of elevated architectural features from which to admire the views provides an important clue to the garden's original appearance as well as to its use. It was conceived as a procession of set pieces, in which visitors were wooed and wowed by the spectacle of nature tamed, but did not so much as ruffle their silk robes in the

process. The grand belvedere gateway on the western perimeter wall gives an elevated view across the whole of the garden towards the east and was admired even before the villa was completed by Montesquieu on his travels through the region in a *burchiello*. From another, exedra-shaped, belvedere situated in the heart of the grounds, six avenues radiate out from under each of the six open arches, each framing a different perspective view at ground level. Higher perspective views are visible from the upper floor, reached by a spiral staircase that winds up a turret to a circular viewing terrace decorated with a balustrade and statues. Additional panoramic views of the park were provided by the coffee house, a small, temple-like pavilion set atop the artificial mound of the ice house, now smothered romantically by the surrounding trees. It originally cut a very fine, if bare, figure with its flight of stone steps set into four monumental steps of clipped box. Cool currents of air from the underground cavity below were conducted through vents to provide welcome relief from the unrelenting heat of summer.

LEFT Spiral staircases wind up the columns of the monumental belvedere gateway admired by Montesquieu in 1728.
ABOVE Height was everything in this garden on the plain. The coffee house offered refreshment as well.
RIGHT Looking through the exedra across the garden towards the belvedere on the garden's western boundary.

The third and westernmost section of the park has been the most transformed by subsequent interventions, so that the original scheme of five distinct zones – one a lawn with a statue, another with a stone table and bench and so on – has been lost. A wooded area was created here in the early nineteenth century, with winding paths and an ice house disguised as a hillock out of which stone busts eerily emerge from a simulated lava flow.

The villa was bought by Napoleon in 1807 and gifted to his viceroy Eugène de Beauharnais but after Waterloo it became Austrian territory and was used by various members of the Habsburg royal family. It was during their occupancy that large trees such as lime and plane were allowed to grow, destroying much of the original

LEFT Flag irises and *Rosa banksiae* growing with abandon in an area originally dedicated to box topiary.
ABOVE The wrought-iron dome of this nineteenth-century pavilion may have been intended as support for climbing plants.
BELOW An area of dense woodland in the northwest corner of the park springs the occasional lugubrious surprise.
RIGHT Gnarled tree roots contribute to these disturbing visions from the nineteenth-century taste for the grotesque.

design of the previous century, but the new owners also took a great interest in botanical matters, building greenhouses to cultivate subtropical plants and avidly collecting plants, amassing 66 different species of citrus alone. The *vaseria* or *orangerie* was created to show off these specimens.

Its space is enclosed on three sides by a high hornbeam hedge in front of which are ranged eighteen statues of mythological figures. In the centre, two concentric paths are intersected by six straight paths like the spokes of a wheel, an arrangement that reflects the organising principle of the park, only on a smaller scale. Of the resulting symmetrical patches of grass, four are occupied by ancient magnolias and the others by box trees which reinforce and anchor the composition, creating an atmosphere of graceful repose. When the gardener recalls the moment in spring in which his charges begin to flower, a gentle smile spreads over his face, 'Ah, signora, if only you could smell it, you wouldn't believe the sweetness as you come through the gate. You might almost lose your senses. That's the moment when it's all been worthwhile.'

ABOVE Fresh air enters one of Villa Pisani's many greenhouses, where the passion for plants lives on.
RIGHT Some of the citrus vases still bear the Pisani crest and date from before the villa's sale to Napoleon in 1807.

PADUA

ORTO
BOTANICO
DI
PADOVA

I N 1222 STUDENTS AND PROFESSORS OF THE University of Bologna staged a protest at infringements of their academic liberty. This was followed by a mass walkout. Tradition has it that it was their arrival in Padua that gave the impetus for the foundation of Italy's second oldest university. When Padua was annexed to Venice in 1405, its university became the *de facto* university of Venice too, benefiting both from the Republic's wealth and its religious and intellectual freedom. Adopting the motto *Universa Universis Patavina Libertas* (The Freedom of Padua is Universal for All), it rapidly established itself as the principal centre of scientific research in Europe. Here, in the early sixteenth century, attracted by the fame of its medical school, Nicolaus Copernicus pursued the studies in astronomy which, upon the publication of *On the Revolution of the Celestial Spheres* in 1543, would usher in a new era of scientific methodology.

It is entirely appropriate that 1543 was also the year in which the first petition was lodged with the university authorities to create a physick garden, signalling an important evolution in the way medicine was taught and practised. The University of Pisa already had one, founded that same year by the botanist and physician Luca Ghini, and bankrolled by the Duke of Tuscany, Cosimo I de' Medici. A decade earlier, Francesco Bonafede had been appointed *Lector Simplicium*, a newly instituted chair in 'simples' or medicinal plants at the University of Padua's

In the heart of the old city, university buildings and the domes of the Basilica of St Anthony of Padua are visible beyond the north gate of the Orto Botanico.

The translucent thorns of *Rosa sericea* subsp. *omeiensis* f. *pteracantha*, a rose introduced from western China in the nineteenth century.

Floating on air-filled leaf stalks, the common water hyacinth, *Eichhornia crassipes*, has spread from the Amazon basin to colonise the world.

medical school. Bonafede believed that it was only by means of practical demonstration with living medicinal plants and other substances of animal and mineral origin that his students could become thoroughly acquainted with their appearance, their properties and their therapeutic use. Together with the pioneering physician Giovanni Battista de Monte, he petitioned first the university authorities and later the Venetian senate for a

> garden of simples, in which, with the help of Venetian navigators, all sorts of medicinal plants, trees, fruits, minerals and other drugs might be brought from far and wide, from the cities of their dominions and especially from Candia [in Crete] and Cyprus, where the Romans obtained their spices, as well as from other parts of the world. And that in said garden a spicery be established that would serve as an index of the dried goods from the Levant, in order to learn to distinguish true medicines from false…

Bonafede's reference to the spice trade was inspired, for this was a subject close to Venice's commercial heart and perhaps never closer than at this time. After the fall of

Constantinople in 1453, Venice's eastern Mediterranean empire had been increasingly subjected to challenge by the Ottomans, and following Vasco da Gama's successful rounding of the Cape of Good Hope in 1498, her lucrative trade with the Far East also hung in the balance. Columbus's recent discovery of the American continent had made it even more obvious that the balance of maritime power was shifting towards those nations with shores on the Atlantic. In the meantime, explorers were bringing back new plants that might be exploited in unimaginable ways. Keeping the University of Padua's medical school abreast of innovations could certainly do no harm, especially since students were flocking from all over Europe to attend it and this was in itself a good source of revenue. On 29 June 1545 the Venetian senate swiftly authorised the purchase of land in Padua for a public garden in which simples could be 'planted, ordered and preserved'. Within a week, terms were agreed for the rent of two irregularly shaped hectares, girded on two sides by the Alicorno canal, belonging to the Benedictine monastery of Santa Giustina near the Basilica of Saint Anthony, in the heart of Padua.

The growing of herbs and their distillation in order to obtain substances used in the treatment of illnesses had long been the preserve of monasteries. Emblematic in this sense was the Vatican's *Viridarium novum* begun in 1279 for the use of the physicians attending Pope Nicolas III. The history of collecting plants for the purposes of study may be traced back to antiquity, to Aristotle and his pupil Theophrastus in the third century BC. Pliny the Elder records a garden at Rhodes in his *Natural History*, while in eleventh-century Moorish Spain, Toledo and Seville both had botanic gardens, founded by the Arab physician Ibn Wafid and botanist Ibn Bassal respectively. The Greek, Latin, Jewish and Arab roots of Mediterranean culture combined in the early fourteenth-century treatise on medicinal plants by Matteo Silvatico, who based his teaching at the medical school of Salerno on his own botanic collection.

At Padua, as indeed elsewhere, knowledge of the plants that constituted the physician's dispensary relied heavily on antique sources such as *On the Materia Medica* by the first-century Greek physician Dioscorides, a canonical text that contained descriptions of animals, minerals and over 500 plants. Despite its limited scope and the numerous errors that had crept in as a result of repeated copying throughout the medieval period, it was still the most influential pharmacopoeia, upon which all others were based. In 1478 the first of numerous printed editions of the *Materia* was published and it remained in circulation for another century, often with scholarly commentaries and additions. But its inadequacies in the age of Leonardo and Dürer, whose extraordinarily precise botanical studies relied on a close observation of nature, were becoming increasingly apparent. It was inconceivable that the art of medicine should still be based on the identification of plant species from ever more fuzzy woodcuts.

One of the reasons that Venice was keen to invest in research of a botanical kind was her near-monopoly of the components of medicinal compounds, including one of the best-selling drugs of the time, the legendary panacea known as Teriaca. It was obtained from pounding the boiled flesh of female vipers with sixty or so assorted

herbs and spices, roots, barks and opium, then liquefying it by the addition of honey and Malvasia wine. Prepared annually at a quasi-magical public ceremony, it was recommended by physicians for everything from a sore throat to the plague, and demand for it continued until the late eighteenth century. Every major city in Italy produced its own Teriaca but that of Venice, undisputed centre of the spice trade, was considered superior. The huge demand for fresh supplies of medicinal plants may also be illustrated by the fact that almost as soon as Padua's new botanic garden was completed, thieves broke in and stole

RIGHT Refashioned in 1704, the gateposts were embellished with acroteria containing wrought-iron plants of fritillary, yucca, pineapple and lily.

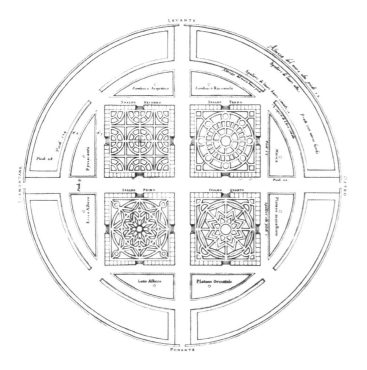

by Vitruvius as the two most perfect of all geometrical figures: the circle and the square. During the Renaissance this combination also took on a special significance as the basis for an ideal system of proportion. The Orto was thus conceived as a visual representation of harmony and perfection, a microcosm of the cosmological ordering of the universe.

The circle had long been a symbol of earthly paradise, and the square inscribed within it lent itself to multiple subdivisions of the number four, which itself carried potent symbolic meanings. Two wide intersecting paths corresponding to the four points of the compass divide the square into quadrants, each of which is arranged in a different geometrical pattern by means of the stone-lined compartments containing the plants. In the eighteenth century, the quadrants (or *spalti*) were modified slightly when the whole site was raised in order to protect against

the freshly planted specimens. A high, circular wall was built around it after this, in 1552, to which a stone inscription in Latin was affixed (a copy of which remains), threatening penalties ranging from fines to exile for anyone caught interfering with or removing plants.

The design was entrusted to the Venetian noble and humanist scholar Daniele Barbaro, together with Pietro da Noale, a professor of medicine. Barbaro, who would later translate Vitruvius's *De Architectura* and commission with his brother Marcantonio a villa at Maser from Palladio (see page 131), was strongly influenced by Roman precedents and among his unrealised plans were a labyrinth, rows of trees with a hippodrome running through the middle, as well as re-creations of specific habitats for plants, such as a valley, a mountain and a plain. The intention was clearly to create a miniature world that would also be a *bella fabbrica*, or beautiful construct. In the end, the encyclopedic nature of the enterprise was proclaimed in a design that sublimated these ideals by means of pure geometry, and specifically those described

ABOVE An engraving from G. Porro, *L'horto de i semplici di Padova*, 1591, shows the intricately ordered design of each quadrant.
RIGHT Still keeping an eye on things … the busts of past prefects look down from the perimeter wall.

flooding, but the layout has remained substantially unaltered. Stone compartments are also laid out in the spaces between the circle and the inner square, making the maximum use of the available space and resulting in a complex design that is both intellectually rigorous and aesthetically pleasing. The organisation of the plants, according to their morphology and use, was undertaken by the first prefect, Luigi Anguillara, aided by the Venetian scholar Pietro Antonio Michiel, a remarkable figure who kept his own botanic garden and whose five-volume herbal, written and illustrated between 1553 and 1565, contains descriptions of 1,028 different species of plant.

In 1553, when its first salaried gardener was appointed, the Orto was celebrated by the pioneering French naturalist Pierre Belon as the 'most splendid' of all those he had seen. By 1591 there were 1,168 specimens listed in

its catalogue and in that same year, a pocket-sized manual was published to help students memorise the names of the plants and their numbered positions in each quadrant. Barbaro's aesthetically and philosophically ambitious design, realised by the architect Andrea Moroni, inspired a rash of botanic garden creations in university medical schools around Italy and abroad, notably at Bologna, Leyden and Montpellier. In the early eighteenth century, various decorative elements were added, such as the four monumental entrance gates embellished with handsome acroteria containing exotic plants in wrought iron and the ornamental balustrade running around the top of the enclosing wall in which are inserted the busts of past Orto prefects. Fountains were erected at the centre of each of the quadrants and later also just outside the wall, one at the south gate dominated by a statue of Theophrastus, the father of botany, and another at the east gate by a statue of Solomon surrounded by busts of the four seasons. In the nineteenth century, permanent greenhouses, classrooms and laboratories were built along the north side, along with a semicircular 'botanic theatre' which is still in use. The

LEFT The Orto Botanico was an outdoor classroom. Each stone-lined quadrant was numbered and labelled to facilitate memorisation.
ABOVE White oleander in Pier Antonio Michiel's *I cinque libri di piante*. The reclining figures probably allude to the plant's toxic properties.

arboretum surrounding the outer wall, which had been established in the previous century was landscaped in the fashionable 'English' style, acquiring winding paths and an artificial mound or belvedere.

As the study of plants evolved into the modern science of botany, the Orto Botanico evolved with it, although its medical beginnings are still apparent in those sections dedicated to plants with therapeutic properties. Today the garden houses about 6,000 plants, some of which are of great age: the so-called Goethe palm (*Chamaerops humilis arborescens*) which inspired his 1790 essay on the metamorphosis of plants, was in fact already old when the German poet visited, having been planted in 1585. Goethe would also have been able to see a *Ginkgo biloba* and one of Europe's first *Magnolia grandiflora*.

Despite its relatively small size, the Orto Botanico has remained faithful to its original didactic and scientific aims: there are sections dedicated to rare and endangered plants of the Triveneto region, alpine and peat-bog flora, and Mediterranean maquis flora, as well as single-genus collections and thematic collections like the poisonous plants or carnivorous plants sections. Near the north gate, two large ponds support a rich collection of exotic aquatic plants that thrive outdoors all year round thanks to a thermal water supply originating from a 300 metre-deep artesian well.

One particularly affecting section is dedicated to those plants introduced for the first time to Italy by way of Paduan soil. Many of the first specimens came from Venice's Byzantine possessions, such as *Syringa vulgaris* (lilac) in 1565, or *Hyacinthus orientalis* in 1590, while a labelled and dated procession of *Agave americana* from Mexico in 1561, *Helianthus annuus* (sunflower) and *Solanum tuberosum* (potato), both introduced in 1590 from the Americas, are testament to Spanish voyages of exploration. Revolutionary changes to European flora,

eating habits and plant fashions are all documented in this unprepossessing row of introduced plants which include *Sesamum indicum* (sesame, 1590), *Robinia pseudoacacia* (1601), *Cedrus deodara* (Himalayan cedar, 1828), *Freesia refracta* (1842) and *Aspidistra elatior* (1845).

The Orto Botanico is a living testament to man's endeavour to explore, his compulsion to classify and, movingly, his instinct to cure, although perhaps not quite in the way envisaged by Thomas Coryat who, on a visit in 1608, was struck by his first sight of an oriental plane:

> Among the rest I saw a certaine rare tree whereof I have often read both in Virgil and in other Authours, but never saw it till then. It is called in Latin Platanus,

[…] which signifieth broade, because he doth extend his boughs very far in breadth […] In English, we call it the Plane tree. It was of goodly height. The poets do faine that Jupiter dallied with Europa under this kind of tree. And it was in former times so highly esteemed amongst the Romans by reason of the shadow, that they were wont sometimes to nourish the roote of it with wine poured about it.

He could not have guessed that within just a few years, the hybrid *Platanus* × *hispanica* would be taking to the streets of London like a native born.

LEFT The wrinkly round leaves of *Euryale ferox* Salisb. from Eastern Asia share a pond with a tall stand of *Cyperus papyrus* from tropical Africa.
ABOVE About fifty poisonous plant species, both cultivated and wild, grow in this area by the west gate.

VILLA BARBARIGO PIZZONI ARDEMANI

VALSANZIBIO

A QUIET COUNTRY ROAD WINDS ROUND the foot of the thickly wooded Euganean hills, skirting the modern village of Valsanzibio. Tucked in behind it on the flat plain is a nine-hole golf course and thermal spa resort. The only sign of what lies up ahead is the name of the road: via Diana. Suddenly, a monumental arched gateway comes into view, straddling a rush-filled pool at the side of the road. On the still surface of the water are mirrored the reflections of two rusticated plinths with youths bearing armorial shields and four blue and white striped mooring poles of the Venetian variety.

The mooring poles are a picturesque reminder of the unique geography of this place, a former marshland that was slowly transformed from malaria-infested swamp into some of the richest and most productive farmland in Italy. Navigable canals once cut through it, all the way from Venice, so in theory it is possible that one might once have arrived here by boat, as Portia's suitors do in the 2004 film version of *The Merchant of Venice*, in which a digitally enhanced Valsanzibio appears as Shakespeare's Belmont, 'the seat of Portia, on the Continent'. The fourteen-hectare Baroque garden of Villa Barbarigo at Valsanzibio, which lies on gently sloping land at the foot of a steep little valley surrounded by woods, was an inspired choice for the dreamlike home of the rich heiress, at one remove from the cares of the city. Its name is a corruption of

Water fore and aft: the monumental watergate of Diana seen from the road with the succession of fish ponds rising gently behind.

Sant'Eusebio, the saint to whom the local twelfth-century church is dedicated.

The Barbarigo family, who acquired the villa and lands of Valsanzibio in the early sixteenth century, were fairly typical of the new Venetian landowning class. Originally merchants, they continued through years of deepening crisis for Venice's maritime empire, to ply trade with the East, but supplementary sources of income such as property and moneylending ensured that when, for example, in 1645 they lost the *Barbarigo* and its entire cargo of Egyptian linen and sugar to Turkish pirates, they did not face financial ruin.

By then a garden had already existed around the villa for at least a century, its delights extolled in 1540 by the Sienese philosopher Alessandro Piccolomini, who completed his astronomical work *Della Sfera del Mondo* there. Two of the fish ponds that have survived to the present day date from this earlier garden. Throughout the latter part of the seventeenth century, Zuane Francesco Barbarigo extended the property, buying up parcels of land from neighbours and diverting local springs in order to supply the numerous fountains and water tricks that were being planned for the new garden. The garden's long

gestation is documented in numerous letters between Zuane Francesco's two sons: Gregorio (1625–97), a devout churchman who became Bishop of Padua in 1664 and was canonised in the twentieth century, and Antonio (1630–1702), who followed in his father's footsteps with a political career in the Venetian republic, eventually becoming a procurator of St Mark's.

As young children, the brothers lost their mother to the plague that decimated Venice's population in 1630–31. They spent many of their formative years at Valsanzibio and the ascetically-inclined Gregorio often went on spiritual retreats to a neighbouring hermitage up in the hills. He entered the priesthood in 1655, and was soon called to Rome as secretary to Pope Alexander VII, where he encountered the work of architect and sculptor Luigi Bernini (1612–81), brother of the more famous Gian Lorenzo, commissioning from him a garden in Rome with fountains. It is thought that Luigi Bernini, who was a water engineer, also played a significant role in designing

ABOVE View from the villa down the garden's main axis, made to look longer by the simple expedient of gradually narrowing the central grass strip.
RIGHT The sheltered garden of Valsanzibio was also famed for its cultivation of rare plants, amongst which were double stocks.

the garden at Valsanzibio, though no drawings survive. Gregorio's involvement in the planning of Valsanzibio is especially intriguing, for he was an austere figure who hated the excesses of the papal court. Yet the garden that took shape over thirty years, between 1661 when the Gate of Diana was built and 1696 when the Rabbit Island was completed, was as sumptuous as anything built by his Roman counterparts.

The search for compromise between such opposing philosophies, and the tension between the classical culture of an educated elite to which the Barbarigo belonged and the renewed religious fervour of a post-Counter Reformation Church is perhaps what makes Valsanzibio especially interesting. The allegorical significance of the garden is still a subject of debate, with theories ranging from the Church's triumph over the pagan world to a less dramatic reconciliation of Christian doctrine with the classical ideals of Greece and Rome, to an initiatory path that conducts the visitor from darkness to a state of enlightenment. It is certain that the garden's complex and

allusive iconographical scheme was inspired by Gregorio, while the practicalities of managing the teams of labourers, artisans, sculptors, stonemasons and hydraulic engineers were ably and somewhat hawkishly attended to by the pragmatic Antonio.

The goddess Diana dominates the gateway to the garden, brandishing her spear while her hunting dogs wait below and two deer on the broken pediment stand alert. As protectress of woodlands, hunting and wild animals, Diana's presence here may seem self-explanatory, but she also had many contradictory attributes: she was a symbol both of chastity and fertility, goddess of the moon and of darkness, she could represent the contemplative life and yet she was a ruthless killer. Statues of Endymion and Actaeon, youths of classical mythology whose association with Diana destroyed them, stand in niches on the portal's façade below. This is decorated with hunting trophies in bas-relief. Originally, the arch on which Diana stands was part of a drum supporting a cupola that had a weathervane on top in the form of a small metal figure of Fame, but this collapsed in the eighteenth century. The arch is built of trachyte quarried in nearby Monselice, while the statues are carved in the whiter and more finely-grained medium of Istrian stone.

Beyond this portal, and visible through the central gateway of wrought iron, is a spectacular vista of water that seems to flow down from the hills beyond, stopping on its way to spray high jets that glitter in the sunlight, to spout obliquely from stone fountains, course over boulders and, finally, pool in silent ripples across the dark surface of the first of a series of long fish ponds. This other-wordly vision is intensified by high walls of clipped box that line the sloping pathways and steps on either side, and by the presence of sculptural groups arranged across the line of sight.

Originally built to ensure a supply of fresh fish to the villa, the fish ponds were endowed with allegorical significance by the addition of statues. Just below Diana's gate, the reclining gods of the Bacchiglione and the Brenta, Padua's two main rivers, empty their water jars into the first pond, home to two graceful black swans. Beyond is

A view of the fish ponds from the viewing gallery on top of Diana's watergate. The labyrinth is surrounded by high hedges on the left.

the first of the garden's fountains, the Rainbow Fountain,
so-called because of the colours formed in the sunlight
when the four spurts of water directed by putti from
captive dolphins' mouths converge in the central jet.
Originally, this shot out of the upturned beak of a dying
swan and the fountain was surrounded by statues representing the Liberal Arts which have since disappeared. The
second fish pond, at a slightly higher level, is dominated
by a sculptural group with Aeolus at its centre, in Greek
mythology the ruler of the wind. Accompanied by a
nymph, he sits over the entrance to a cave, out of which
water cascades over steps. To his left is Boreas, old and
craggy as befits the north wind, while perched on a rock
to his right is the youthful Zephyrus, the west wind.

Above this, at the intersection of the garden's two main
axes, the Pila Fountain gushes. While one axis is formed
by the waterway of three fish ponds, the other stretches
almost the whole breadth of the little valley, from the
wooded southern boundary of the garden, along the *tapis
vert* that runs between towering box hedges forming an
ever-widening avenue up to the villa and then beyond,

its progress marked by a double row of cypresses that
climb the steep hill behind. Four sculptures by Enrico
Marengo (active 1680), whose workshop produced most of
the garden's stonework and statuary, are arranged around
the octagonal Pila Fountain: the male figures of Argo
and Mercury on the left, and two female allegorical figures
representing Health and Fecundity on the right. Like all
the statuary at Valsanzibio, they bear cryptic inscriptions
in Italian that comment on their symbolism, or, according
to some scholars, add a political or philosophical slant
to their meaning.

Today, the suggested itinerary is rather different
from that envisaged by the original planners. One of the
features for which Valsanzibio is most famous is its square
boxwood labyrinth and it is to this that the visitor, having
entered the garden by a small gate in the southeast corner,
is directed first, after a brief diversion through periwinkle-

LEFT The fleeting nature of human life is alluded to in this statue of Time
who kneels, despairing of his burden, clutching an hourglass in his left hand.
ABOVE Four putti perch on the edge of the Rainbow Fountain, exchanging
glances like players in a quartet.

carpeted woodland. The labyrinth has a central belvedere that may be accessed directly. Then, having studied the layout and become enlightened, the visitor descends and must try to find his way out by a different route from the one by which he entered. Having completed this rite, he may want to contemplate the choice that was denied Gregorio Barbarigo by his ambitious father: a hermit's cave sits in its own plot of ground, complete with monolithic stone lintels.

Once, the hedges that enclosed the garden's various regularly spaced sections were clipped low so that it was possible to see the whole layout at a glance. The eighteenth-

century Romantic taste for a more natural informality also reached Valsanzibio, with the not unpleasing result that new vistas are constantly opening up through gaps and corridors in the thickly planted vegetation. Although this was not the original intention, it means that certain sections remain hidden from view until the last moment and are, for precisely that reason, all the more affecting. This is the case of the monumental statue of Time, whose crouching form is met suddenly, in a secluded woodland glade. Wings half-folded and head turned to glance off to his left, he seems just to have landed, or to be about to take off again, and though his burden is heavy, he cannot stay. If he symbolises transcendence, his counterpart is to be found in the symmetrical section opposite, on the other side of the main garden axis.

BELOW LEFT Closer inspection of Flora sets off concealed water tricks.
BELOW RIGHT Opposite Flora, the blinded Cyclops, Polyphemus, has a rock ready to hurl at Odysseus's ship.

The trapped inhabitants of the oval Rabbit Island that rises elegantly from a wide moat, surrounded by its own low box hedge, seem untroubled by their use as symbols of immanence. They hop in and out of the tunnels beneath a rustic gazebo all summer long, busily active in ways only to be expected from such obvious symbols of fertility. To keep them company, an aviary in the form of a cupola sits atop the gazebo, while large carp lurk in the greenish shallows.

ABOVE LEFT The *leporarium*, a common feature of classical gardens, was an entertaining method of securing a source of fresh meat.
ABOVE The rabbit island in an engraving by G. Campana, from D. Rossetti, *Le fabbriche e i giardini dell'Ecc.ma Casa Barbarigo*, 1702.
BELOW This sonnet informs the visitor that he is on the threshold of paradise, at which point he receives a soaking from hidden water jets.

As it nears the villa, the central avenue broadens out majestically at the Fountain of Flowers, where an inscription warns the unwary that wickedness is sometimes found where least expected. Just up ahead are the threatening figures of blinded Polyphemus and boulder-throwing Typhon, contrasted by the harmonious forms of Flora and the earth goddess Ops. But we sit on the stone benches to puzzle over the moral of this juxtaposition at our peril. Powerful jets of water periodically arc into the air from all directions, their aim still keen despite the passage of centuries. Evil is mocked by the life-giving force of water.

The Fountain of Enlightenment with its viscid mushroom-cap top, our final goal, remains just out of reach. Spaced around it, eight statues celebrate the art and virtues of agriculture. A flight of seven beautifully inscribed

steps is guarded on either side by two lithe stone panthers, momentarily distracted by thirst. Beyond the balustrade, the private garden is a geometric fantasy of box topiary.

Whatever its precise symbolic meaning, the sensual joys offered by this little paradise have long been known and appreciated. One scholarly account of 1931 enthused:

> Is there a native of Padua who doesn't know Valsanzibio? Is there a young man alive who has not laughed of a summer's day to see their fiancée jump up screaming as she is soaked by jets of water, then rush up the flight of steps only to stop short as another curtain of water blocks her escape, so that she is trapped, unable even to beg for mercy?

ABOVE The Fountain of Revelation is reached at last, in the form of a glistening stone mushroom in front of the villa.
LEFT Centuries of damp have blackened this feline's pelt, yet a ferocious thirst still vanquishes his fierce nature.

VILLA PISANI
BOLOGNESI SCALABRIN
VESCOVANA

NOTHING ON THE ROAD MAP PREPARES the eye for the ravaged, low-lying plain that is the Basso Padovano between Este and Rovigo. Almost bare of trees and featureless but for hulks of unidentifiable industrial units and giant pylons, it seems the quintessence of a non-place, to be traversed as rapidly as its wide, empty roads will allow. Occasionally, the former lords of this floodplain, the Adige and Gorzone rivers, burst their high banks, but for now they are safely confined, coursing invisibly towards the Adriatic.

After the Venetian Republic drained these insalubrious marshlands in the sixteenth and seventeenth centuries, thousands of men and teams of oxen were put to work to break up the silt-rich but virgin soil. Now, the vast fields are gaunt and unending, criss-crossed by mile upon mile of deep ditches mechanically dug and shaven of any growth. What garden can possibly have sprung up in such a monotonous, bleak and unpromising land as this?

Vescovana, oasis-like, announces itself from a distance with its bell tower and a dark smudge of green that turns out to be the high profiles of trees growing in the garden of Villa Pisani Bolognesi Scalabrin. A long, low, ochre house sits with its back to what passes for the village square. In the bar the talk is of matters agricultural. Yes, the entrance to the villa is just there, a small brown door in the wall running along one side of the street, easily overlooked.

LEFT 'A delicious air, a bath of sunlight full of the sounds of morning birds, and the scent of flowers, streams through your window.'

ABOVE True to Villa Pisani tradition, vases of lemon trees are still moved outside to adorn the garden each spring.

That evening Margaret was stunned by the myriad perfumes floating in on the damp night air, and captivated by the countess's unique blend of Eastern sensuousness and love of comfort, of French refinement and what she recognised as a strong English instinct to temper and soften the natural environment. Recalling her first impressions of the garden, she wrote:

> You see around you a southern garden full of roses which fascinate your northern eye. The size and scent of the magnolias charm you, and the delicious lavishness of sweet-pea hedges. The sleepy moat, overgrown with water-lilies and pink tamarisk, delights you, for here a gondola lies hidden under syringa-trees; the singing of the birds, the groves of poplar and of pine, and the little arbour on a hill all sweetly scented with honeysuckle, where a red terra-cotta Madonna has her shrine – these things entrance you more than the botanical specimens which have cost so much thought and care.

Her book is a spirited and affectionate chronicle of Italian rural life in one of the last feudal holdings of northern Italy, containing descriptions of day trips to such places as Arquà and the Castle of Catajo and to the famous villa gardens of Valsanzibio and Trissino. But it is above all a deeply sympathetic portrait of the autocratic, charming and eccentric countess who became her lifelong friend and who, in the midst of a melancholy plain and hampered by an uncompromising climate and an often uncomprehending workforce, created one of the most beautiful and unusual gardens of its time in Italy, joyfully sharing its sensual delights with anybody who was interested enough to appreciate it.

The hostess who welcomed the little party of English visitors on that spring night was the childless widow of the Pisani doge's grandson, Almorò III Pisani. She was then fifty-seven, a still handsome woman, well-read and intellectually curious who conversed wittily and brilliantly in several European languages and had a gregarious, generous nature that found an outlet in hosting as many

It was not at this dusty side entrance but rather at the main door on the north side with its statue-lined gravel sweep that, on a warm May night in 1888, a young Englishwoman arrived from Venice in the company of her father and some friends to pay a visit to a new acquaintance, a certain Countess Evelina Pisani. It had been a five-hour journey, but to nineteen-year-old Margaret it seemed a fairy-tale, the romantic impressions of which later inspired her to write an eloquent account. *Days Spent on a Doge's Farm* was published in 1893, the title being, as she readily admitted, somewhat misleading, for the doge in question, Alvise Pisani, had died in 1741 without ever having set foot in the place.

Margaret Symonds was the daughter of the bohemian poet and scholar of the Italian Renaissance John Addington Symonds and his wife Catherine, sister of the indomitable botanical illustrator Marianne North. Margaret had enjoyed an unorthodox childhood. No secret had ever been made of the fact that their household included Addington's lover, a Venetian gondolier.

ABOVE Evelina van Millingen in an Ottoman-inspired bridal gown. Her penchant for such costumes earned her the unflattering epithet of 'La Turchetta'. RIGHT One of the stone peacocks, decorated for a wedding party in the villa garden.

of the diverse and cosmopolitan people encountered in Venice as she could persuade to travel out to Vescovana. She had taken to spending long periods in the country, although by happy coincidence her town house was in Palazzo Barbaro on the Grand Canal, the top floors of which were lived in during the 1880s by a wealthy Boston couple, Daniel and Ariana Curtis.

The arrival of the Curtises had injected a new, transatlantic energy into the Venetian expatriate community. Henry James was a regular visitor, while John Singer Sargent was a close friend of the Curtis's painter son Daniel and for a time had a studio there. Other frequent guests were James McNeill Whistler, William Merritt Chase, Robert Browning, Vernon Lee, Isabella Stewart Gardner, Edith Wharton, Bernard Berenson... and John Addington Symonds.

But there was more to the Countess Pisani than drawing-room muse. After the death of her husband, she had single-handedly taken on the running of the vast estates that constituted her livelihood. She seemed to relish the task, though nothing in her upbringing could

have prepared her for such a role. Teresa Evelina Berengaria van Millingen was born in Constantinople in 1831, the daughter of Marie Dejean and Julius van Millingen, a young English doctor of Dutch descent who had attended Lord Byron during his last illness. Her mother was of French, Armenian and Greek extraction and fifteen when Millingen made her his wife. The marriage foundered and the three children were sent to Rome. They barely saw their mother for Marie Dejean led a nomadic, adventurous and somewhat scandalous life which she recounted in *Thirty Years in the Harem*, 1872. Evelina was never reconciled with her absent mother.

As a young woman Evelina lived with her father in Constantinople but during a visit to Venice she met and married the already middle-aged Almorò. He, according to Venetian society hostess Lady Enid Layard, was a 'miserable looking little man' who 'went about with a small monkey in his breast pocket', but he was also a scion of the illustrious and immensely profligate Pisani family. In his youth he had watched helplessly as his father and uncles were eventually forced to sell the magnificent Villa Pisani at Stra, together with its important coin collection, library and paintings. From his family inheritance, Almorò III had salvaged Villa Pisani at Vescovana.

The Vescovana villa was first and foremost a farmhouse, built on the ruins of a medieval watchtower and enlarged in the early sixteenth century by Francesco Pisani, the Bishop of Padua, who also commissioned the Villa dei Vescovi in nearby Luvigliano. Originally a fief of the Ferrarese Estensi, the lands passed first to Padua and in 1405 to the Venetian Republic. Then, as part of a policy of territorial expansion instituted when Venice's maritime influence began to falter in the fifteenth century, they were auctioned off to Venetian patrician families.

Long, arcaded *barchesse* were built on either side of the central, three-storey portion of the house to accommodate the out-buildings necessary for a large-scale agricultural enterprise. In the eighteenth century, the land on the south side of the house had an orchard, with a large space devoted to citrus cultivation, for here, as elsewhere in the region, the production of peaches, flowers, lemons and citrons represented an important source of income: at one point, a thousand peach trees were registered on the Vescovana property. The tender citrus plants were sheltered from bitter

winter frosts and fogs by a structure that could be assembled and removed as the need arose, and the account books inform us rather touchingly that the gardener from Stra came over specially to see to this task.

When the young countess arrived in 1852, she found a bare, uncomfortable, exposed house, unshaded, unsheltered and unadorned by any garden. The large rooms on the first floor were used for drying beans and laundry and storing wood, while the ground floor was barely habitable, with passing pigs making frequent incursions. This was despite the fact that in the sixteenth century the interiors had been decorated by some of the most fashionable painters of the day, including Paolo Veronese. Evelina set about enclosing a small garden space around the north side of the house, thus imposing a distinctly un-Italian separation of private and public space. But it was on the south side that she lavished her prodigious energies, first by delineating the perimeter of her five-hectare plot with a dense planting of trees including white poplars, catalpas, oaks, planes, sweet chestnuts and sequoias and then by laying out a formal garden with box hedges and sculpture according to an elaborate and elegant scheme that owed much of its inspiration to English Victorian tastes. Evelina had never been to England but she sent for her seeds and bulbs from English companies and seems to have kept up with the latest works of English garden theorists. In 1892 she rapidly incorporated, to the disapproval of her young English friend, some of the ideas of Reginald Blomfield as expressed in his just-published *The Formal Garden in England*. In typically hyperbolic style, Margaret commented:

> We were forced to drag our weary limbs upon the balcony, and peering into the most absolute darkness with dusty eyes, to declare we saw marvels in the garden, where, as a fact, nothing was visible save fireflies. In the morning, however, miracles were disclosed – innumerable mockeries met our eyes (Mr Blomfield, by the by, ought to feel flattered, for his book has made havoc in a Lombard plot of

Mid-summer morning light steals over the flower-filled garden, seen to its best advantage from the balcony on the first floor.

ground.) Half the old field has been turned into a "formal garden" and christened Crispin de Pass. It is all plotted out with grass, and gravel paths, and flower beds. Gates, balustrades, and sweet-pea hedges enclose it. Everyone says this arrangement is right, that it gives what was needed to the architecture of the house. But for my part I loved the old way well, and would never have had it thus scratched and blotched over. However, it is splendidly done, and in a year or two it will be overgrown.

Evelina delighted in word play and all the parts of her garden were similarly labelled with ironic appellatives. A rockery was referred to as the 'Mockery', possibly on account of the short lifespan of the Alpine plant specimens upon which she and Margaret, mountain-lovers both, lavished so much care. One arbour she called the 'Blue Devils' and the fashionable fake ruins she denominated 'The Temple of Baal' and the 'Walls of Jericho'. A great admirer of the work of Edward Lear, she referred to her lands as 'Gromboolia' ('And reached the great Gromboolian plain'), and must have been amused to discover that Lear had written *The Owl and the Pussycat* for Margaret's older sister Janet. The 'Crispin de Pass'

parterre of which Evelina was so proud, and which is the defining feature of her garden, was a reference to the Dutch engraver Crispin van de Passe whose *Hortus Floridus* of 1614 contains a plate entitled 'Spring' portraying a formal garden of curving, box-lined beds filled with tulips and other spring flowers. In the left foreground of van de Passe's engraving, a man looks out over the scene from behind a balustrade. This inspired Evelina to introduce similar marble balustrades, with the effect of framing certain views or suggesting a stopping place from which to admire the scene.

The ambitious and unusual geometric layout of low, flower-filled beds is best seen from the first floor of the house: two halves of a large, low box-hedge-lined square, each containing a central bed, are intersected by a wide gravel path that leads to the garden's centrepiece, a two-basined fountain of neo-Renaissance design. Behind the fountain the avenue continues in a straight line, surmounted by a high, rose-covered arch, while on either side, more box-lined beds lead off in a symmetrical,

BELOW *Spring*, an engraving from *Hortus Floridus*, 1614, by Crispin van de Passe. Evelina claimed this was the inspiration for the layout of her garden.
RIGHT 'I rose at early hours, and went into the garden when it was yet heavy with dew. How glorious were the roses after sleep!' *Days on a Doge's Farm.*

fan-like arrangement, some filled with grass and others with yew topiary. Around the half-circle that is thus formed beyond the fountain are full-length statues and herms, alternating in the warmer months with large terracotta pots containing lemon trees. Numerous arches with climbing roses are judiciously spaced about the garden, lending height and a graceful unity to the whole design. Further back, the rounded mounds, cones and cubes of clipped yew give way to increasingly informal arrangements of tall trees and flowering shrubs.

Marble sculptures of homely putti and angels, interspersed with characters from the *commedia dell'arte*, peasant girls and herms lend permanency and stillness to the profusion of evergreen forms and the 3,000 or so roses, creating a playful, wistful and informal atmosphere. Low columns bearing baskets of fruit or urns, secluded stone benches nestled under rose bowers and ornamental fountains add to the air of aristocratic ease. Two marble peacocks on either side of the balustrade framing the

garden view from the house recall the countess's Oriental origins and are echoed by two more at the back of the formal garden on square columns. A statue of Margaret Symonds stands a little way back from the central fountain dedicated to her.

Evelina and Almorò rest in the neo-gothic family chapel built within the walls of their beloved garden. On Evelina's death in 1902, the property passed to the Marchese Carlo Bentivoglio d'Aragona and then, through marriage, to the Counts Nani Mocenigo. In the late 1960s it was sold to the Bolognesi Scalabrin family and is still in their possession.

As the little brown door swings open and the immense portico of the *barchessa* stretches out before one, still giving way in its central section to a shady vine pergola and still inhabited by motley dogs, cats and doves, it is difficult not to feel moved by the definite change in the quality of the light and air, and at the vision of a garden that has survived with its charm and its informal elegance intact for almost a hundred and fifty years.

VILLA VALMARANA
(FORMERLY CITTADELLA-VIGODARZERE)
SAONARA

O N   A   H O T   J U L Y   E V E N I N G   I N   1 8 3 8 ,   T H R E E young men set off from Padua in a carriage to visit a fourth friend, Count Andrea Cittadella Vigodarzere, at his villa in the outlying village of Saonara. It was dark when they arrived, but their host ushered them out to the garden nonetheless and had them board a small boat. He then rowed them out onto a vast lake that glowed silver in the moonlight. Above, they could make out the steep slopes of a hill covered in dark trees and a rustic bridge flung across a gully, in the depths of which a stream flowed noiselessly into the lake. Someone pointed out a cave on the shore, its entrance lapped by the moonlit water, and evoked its mythical past as the place where, under a shroud of darkness and mystery, the Knights Templar had carried out their secret rites. Since the countryside to the east of Padua is famously flat and featureless all the way to the nearby southern Venetian lagoon, this must have been a dreamlike experience. As they sat down later to an exquisite supper, the young men praised the architect whose protean vision had afforded them such an affecting experience. His name was Giuseppe Jappelli, and their visit to his Masonic garden had only just begun.

Born in Venice in 1783, Jappelli studied architecture in Bologna before undertaking a career as a hydraulic engineer. In common with many young men of his generation, he was enthusiastic in his support of Napoleon, seeing in the young emperor a force for good that seemed to promise a much-needed political and moral renewal. It was doubtless in this same spirit of hope and belief in the principles of the Enlightenment that he became a member of the Freemasons in 1806. From its

foundation in London in 1717, this secret society had spread rapidly throughout Europe, attracting an essentially radical and anticlerical elite of educated men who found, in the values of fraternity, equality and friendship that the movement propounded, a source of valuable mutual support, both personally and professionally. The establish- ment of Masonic lodges had not been without its vicissitudes in Venice and Padua, but it was largely due to their existence that members of the aristocracy and increasing numbers of the bourgeoisie were able to establish links with the most advanced intellectual and artistic currents in Europe.

In 1809 Jappelli joined the French army and was posted to Lombardy. He resumed his architectural career after the French defeat with the planning of a villa garden in the English style near Cremona. When Lombardy and the Veneto became part of the Habsburg Empire after the Congress of Vienna in 1815, Jappelli returned to Padua and

LEFT Ancient grandeur is suggested by ruined masonry supporting rustic bridges over a man-made gorge in the grounds of Villa Valmarana.
RIGHT *Baptism by Water*. One of the stone relief panels inspired by what Joseph von Hammer-Purgstall claimed were medieval coffer decorations.

received a career-changing commission. The centrepiece of the celebrations to welcome Emperor Francis I of Austria on his first state visit to this distant part of his empire was a fawning spectacle entitled *Feste Euganee*, in which the emperor himself was included in the scenography, appearing as guarantor of the peace and prosperity of Padua under threat from a malicious deity who had taken the form of the river Brenta. For the occasion the main hall of Padua's Palazzo della Regione was transformed by Jappelli into a miniature replica of the Paduan landscape, with the Euganean hills, a river, and an avenue of full-grown poplars forming a backdrop to temples, fountains and a triumphal column around which the dramatic action, with a full cast of dryads, satyrs, fauns and various deities, took place.

Throughout the political upheavals of the previous two decades, the Academy of Sciences, Letters and Arts in Padua had hosted a series of readings and debates on the subject of the new, English style of landscape garden. A quite remarkable group of poets, philosophers and erudite 'gardenists' dedicated themselves to discussing its theoretical and practical implications in the Italian context. There was a certain understandable hostility towards the all-conquering way in which the new fashion had swept through Europe without reference to local or older traditions. The crux of the argument in Padua, however, was whether this new style of landscape garden had any place at all in Italy, and if so, on what terms. Elements of the *giardino all'inglese* had begun to be incorporated into the designs of thoughtful owner-gardeners who enjoyed experimenting with its potential for narratives of emotional intensity. This was an aspect that Giuseppe Jappelli seized upon and, unhindered by the theoretical scruples of an older generation, developed into a distinctive and highly successful style of his own, displaying the bold instinct of the right man in the right place at the right time. The commission to create a garden for his friend and fellow Freemason Count Antonio Vigodarzere came in the wake of Jappelli's triumphant theatricals for the emperor. Once again, he was called upon to design a scenography, but this time, in the flat, arid, workaday countryside of Saonara. Manpower was not lacking: the peasants were on the verge of famine in 1816 and it was Count Antonio's view that the best way of helping them was to offer them remunerative work. There was nothing in the local topography that could be exploited for the transformation of fourteen hectares of featureless farmland into the Romantic garden that Jappelli planned, so work there certainly was.

Around the villa he arranged a series of gently undulating oval lawns surrounded, and sometimes encroached upon, by thickly planted woodland or shrubberies that included tamarisk, lilac and mimosa

LEFT A club-wielding Hercules stands on a summit above the artificial lake, his role in this 'Masonic' garden unexplained.
ABOVE RIGHT Interior of the Templars' chapel. To the left of the main altar is the doorway leading into the chamber of oaths.
RIGHT Against the wall outside the chapel, a tomb has been reassembled, with the bizarre addition of a breastplate covering the head.

fabled role in the building of the Temple of Solomon, made its presence particularly significant.

Today the woods are overgrown and many of the subtleties of Jappelli's original planting have been lost, but it is still possible to share something of the awe experienced by the garden's nineteenth-century visitors. Beyond the villa, a thick swathe of woodland is entered by means of a path that leads over a wooden bridge then winds uphill in a series of loops that confuse the visitor as to the garden's true extent. It then circles the lake and enters a shady avenue, darkened by yew and cypress, at the end of which the gloomy façade of a small gothic church appears, its tracery partly obscured by ivy and its ruined spires poking up through the overhanging branches of the surrounding trees. It was not built as a ruin, but has since become one, although enough of the original decoration survives for its effect to be still appreciated. A contemporary visitor, the writer Tullio Dandolo, entered fully into the spirit of the place with a melodramatic account of what he found there in 1833:

Pushing back the wrought-iron gate there is a screech of hinges and I find myself in a mortuary chapel [...] spaced around in the half-light are tombs, the walls are hung with war trophies, blackened by time, and the reclining figures of the occupants, sculpted on the lids of their caskets, lie awaiting the trumpet-blast of the final summons. Not a flower grows upon their forgotten burial place, their rusty armour creaks as it swings in the wind whistling through crannies [...] rain occasionally floods in over the ruined floor, bats

grouped together for their colouristic effects. But it was in the northwest section that architect and patron gave free rein to their fantasy – and it was here that most of the spadework was required – in the creation of a fantastical landscape revolving around the arcane theme of the Knights Templar. An enormous, deep lake was dug out and the excavated material piled up to form a series of mounds and hills around its banks, the highest of which had a belvedere. From the heights of this latter-day Parnassus, before the trees grew too tall, the domes of Padua's Basilica of Saint Anthony could be seen, and on a clear day the faint glitter of the Venetian lagoon was visible to the northeast. Over 35,000 trees were planted, prominent among them those species symbolising the immortality of the soul. The brooding, melancholic air of yew, box and cypress was contrasted with the dappled trunks of plane and the tremulous leaves of poplar, while acacia's close associations with Freemasonry, due to its

ABOVE One of the grottoes created during the second building phase, through which visitors were led towards the climax of their initiatory journey. The steps descend to the shores of the lake.

BELOW LEFT Restoration of the warren of tunnels and chambers by the side of the lake has, perhaps not inadvertently, created some uncanny effects.
BELOW RIGHT Jappelli used both natural and artificial materials in the attempt to produce a complete sensory experience.

flit in and out at nightfall and nocturnal birds make their nests here; corroding moss has spread like stains over the figures, while upon their features, composed in the stillness of death, I thought I could still see traces of the fierce and prideful passions of yesteryear; the warriors hold tight to their colossal double-edged swords, as if even in death they had not wanted to be separated from their trusty companions.

His initial terror giving way to pity, then finally to an admiring mournfulness at the contemplation of the Templars' fate, Dandolo's emotional involvement was as complete as the artifice of what he described.

Many churches and monasteries in Padua and the surrounding area had been suppressed during Napoleon's short-lived Regno Italico, so there was no shortage of genuine ecclesiastical material with which to create this neo-gothic vision. In the five years between Dandolo's description above and the visit of the three friends alluded to at the beginning of this chapter – in reality a fictional account but one closely according with other contemporary descriptions of the garden – Jappelli continued work on the garden, adding further episodes to the narrative, probably at the instigation of his close friend the young Count Andrea Cittadella who inherited his uncle's property in 1835. While the original idea for the garden at Saonara may have been inspired by François Raynouard's tragedy *Les Templiers*, which related the medieval suppression of the Crusader Order of the Temple, and a translation of which was published in Padua in 1815, the second phase introduced elements that point rather to an elaborate and sensational, but fundamentally light-hearted joke, conceived to arouse a variety of emotions in the visitor and perhaps to sow the seeds of doubt and curiosity. The Knights Templar narrative was continued in a complex of grottoes and interconnecting tunnels built almost twenty years after the garden's inception, between the back of the Templars' chapel and the shores of the lake. By 1838 a door had been inserted by the chapel's altar and the visitor was directed through it on a journey that purported to represent the Masonic path from symbolic death (in the chapel) through the various stages of initiation to final rebirth.

An engraving from a drawing by G.B. Cecchini shows Baphomet in his original place in the grotto, with two mid-nineteenth century visitors.

To this day, Jappelli and Cittadella's true intention remains unclear. Upon coming to power in the Veneto, the Habsburg government had outlawed Freemasonry and the Masonic lodge to which Jappelli belonged was closed down in 1813. Jappelli was forced to abjure his membership to the viceroy in Milan, claiming that it had been an error of youth. Then, in 1818, the Austrian orientalist Joseph von Hammer-Purgstall published a pseudo-historical study written in Latin entitled *Mysterium Baphometis revelatum*, that sought to discredit Freemasonry by claiming that its members were the degenerate heirs to a secret knowledge and magical powers, passed down to them by the last Grand Master of the Order before his execution in 1314. Hammer-Purgstall asserted among other things that the Templars, and by inference, the Freemasons, were only apparently Christians but in fact worshipped a pagan idol called Baphomet. In a subsequent study, *Mémoire sur deux Coffrets gnostiques du moyen-Age, du Cabinet de M. le Duc de Blacas*, published in Paris in 1832, Hammer-Purgstall

reproduced some bas-relief coffer decorations and suggested they had a similar origin to the medieval coffers in the imperial collection of Vienna described in his earlier book. He claimed that they showed a statue of Baphomet and figures engaged in depraved gnostic practices. Two of these naïf images – the Baptism by Fire and the Baptism by Water – were faithfully copied by Jappelli as bas-reliefs and placed in the grotto at Saonara. And yet, by 1835, when Jappelli and his patron began planning the second phase of the garden, they could have been in no doubt that any allusions to Freemasonry would have been anathema to the government of the day.

The door at the back of the chapel opens into an oval room lined with stone benches and a throne for the swearing-in ceremony. Although it is now no longer possible to enter this inner sanctum, it is still partially visible, both from the chapel and from the other side, in the cave where the next stage of the initiation took place: the baptism by fire and by water. The two stone bas-reliefs representing this process are no longer in their original places and of the other Masonic symbols that once reinforced the gnostic message there is no trace, except for a sinister, stretcher-shaped gridiron, presumably for use in the baptism by fire. Originally the grottoes were constructed of masonry and roofed over with wooden beams and laths, to which rough plaster was added to look like natural rock. The domed ceiling of the last remaining

cave is still studded with the hooks that once held up real stalagmites. Light filtered in from tiny openings, reflecting off crystals set into the walls or bouncing off patches of brightly painted azure and vermilion, while drops of water trickled and dripped down from above. As he moved through the semi-darkness, the combination of colours, smells and sounds would have worked on the visitor's senses to enchant and thoroughly confound him, but the climax was still to come.

It was only next day when, rested after a good night's sleep, the three young men resumed their inspection of Andrea Cittadella's garden. From the gothic chapel they proceeded to the oath room, the baptismal room with its seven-pointed star, pelican and large G, and then down a narrow corridor, at the end of which they came face-to-face with the occupant of the final, enormous grotto. Towering above them was a four-metre-high statue of none other than Baphomet, a hermaphrodite pagan idol with beard and breasts, holding aloft the chain of Time. The vision struck orchestrated terror into their souls.

During the Second World War these once considerable structures were bombed and much of the remaining, shattered masonry was carried off by local people desperate to rebuild their homes. As a result, it is now quite difficult to reconstruct in one's mind the extraordinary creation that once stood here. A warren of brick walls, passages and steps surmounts the homely little cottage that now stands on the banks of the lake. Baphomet too was dismantled and carted off, bit by bit. One elderly local witness recalls that even before the war it was sport among the village boys to stone the statue from a hole in the grotto's roof. For his part, Jappelli went on to receive important commissions from both state and private individuals for the rest of a successful career that ended only with his death in 1852. There are few Romantic gardens in the Veneto that are untouched by his scenic genius, but none is as unashamedly arcane and as bizarrely spectacular as that of Villa Cittadella-Vigodarzere, now Valmarana.

ABOVE An elfin presence on a fountain serves as further reminder that in some gardens, all is not always as it seems.
RIGHT Islands in the artificial lake are anchored by the characteristic 'knees' of swamp cypress, the leaves of which turn spectacular shades of red in autumn.

VILLA EMO
RIVELLA DI MONSELICE

THERE ARE FOUR VILLAS BEARING THE name of Emo in the Veneto, but only one has a dog rose scrambling round its gatepost. In a garden that takes its inspiration as much from the wild plants of the surrounding countryside as from elements of the Veneto garden tradition, its presence here is emblematic.

The garden of Villa Emo looks, to all intents and purposes, like a historic garden, for many of the forms and features that have come to be associated with the region's great gardens are to be found here. A formal parterre takes its expected place in front of the villa, and the simple geometry of rectangular rose beds flanked by fish ponds creates a sense of spaciousness and harmony, so that the villa with its high, colonnaded portico seems to sit proudly above the well-ordered symmetry of its grounds. But the visitor quickly comes to realise that these historical elements are quotations from a tradition rather than its embodiment, and that they are here reinterpreted in a spirit of good humour and knowledgeable experiment. Like all the best traditions they have, by definition, been tried and tested and found to work in this particular climate, on this particular soil and under this particular sky, but here they are merely pretexts for a quite different gardening agenda. For this is above all the garden of someone who loves plants and who revels in the colours and patterns and scents of growing things, whether they be wild strays that have self-seeded or the latest cultivars from a long-pondered catalogue.

Built in 1588, the villa is attributed to Palladio's close follower Vincenzo Scamozzi (1548–1616) who, unlike the older architect, had much to say about the design of gardens, giving voice to his ideas in a treatise of 1615

Looking towards the entrance gates. Rising and falling rhythms of wrought iron, stucco and mop-headed hydrangeas.

entitled *Idea dell'architettura universale*. Although nothing is known of what, if anything, he laid out around this imposing white stucco villa with its deeply scalloped walls decorated with ball finials extending out on either side of its square body, it is probable that there would originally have been a landing stage from the canal just outside the main entrance and a formal garden leading to the front steps of the villa.

Canals were the preferred way for the nobility to reach their country possessions from the city, and the Canale Bisatto (the name derives from the dialect word for the once abundant eel that inhabited its waters), now flowing between embankments so high that the villa is partially hidden from view, has an interesting history. It was cut

in the twelfth century in order to provide Vicenza with a direct outlet to the Adriatic by way of the deviated Bacchiglione river, with the express intention also of depriving rival Padua of the water she needed to run her mills and keep her own waterways viable. The so-called Water Wars dragged on for three centuries until annexation by the Venetian Republic finally put an end to the matter, but in the meantime a complex network of canals had been built on the *terraferma*, providing a valuable transport network for men and materials. At Longare, where the Bisatto canal began, blocks of the renowned white Vicenza stone could be loaded on boats and floated down to Venice for shaping into buildings and sculpture, while the excellent trachyte, quarried in

the Euganean hills, was for several centuries ferried to Venice in enormous quantities to be used in sea defences and to pave the city's streets.

The garden of Villa Emo is constantly refreshed and vivified by the sight and sound of running water, an impression that begins at the front gates where water deviated from the canal runs in a bubbling torrent along a ditch to the side. A row of *Populus pyramidalis* or Lombardy poplars screens the villa from the occasional cyclist pedalling slowly along the towpath and from the

LEFT The parterre's bold design was laid out half a century ago and is subtly asymmetrical. Beyond the screen of poplars is the canal embankment. BELOW Behind the villa on the left is the magnolia avenue, with the pale line of the Euganean hills visible beyond.

noise of traffic on the busy road beyond. At their roots, mare's tail pokes its primitive spikes up among violets in early spring, and clumps of yellow flag iris alternate with the unfurling leaves of cuckoo pint. Wild honeysuckle tangles with ivy on the steep canal bank beyond the ditch. To the left, the poplars are planted in a double row, forming a long avenue that stretches to the southwest corner. Their presence defines a large part of the garden, for wherever the seething sound of their leaves reaches, there is the impression of a cooling breeze passing through the air, even on those days when the griddle-like heat of the sky seems to shrivel every living thing to exhausted immobility.

When Countess Giuseppina Emo and her husband Andrea began in the 1960s to transform the farmland and

orchards around the villa into a garden, they discovered the buried remains of two long fish ponds. Now restored and incorporated into the design, these handsome ribbons of water uniting the front garden with the back seem at first sight symmetrical, but in fact are subtly different. While that on the left is lined with stone walls, the earth banks of the pond on the right descend naturally towards the water's edge and the resultant masses of buttercups and forget-me-nots reflected in the water create a haze of brightness that makes the thousands of pale purple iris seem to float above them. Pond life pullulates and croaks, the iridescent blue of the quivering damselfly is here

LEFT The spectacular flowering of the fragrant, five-petalled *Rosa gigantea* on a farm annexe.
BELOW A paulownia's tubular blossom adds a note of pale amethyst to an already richly chromatic arrangement.

and gone in an instant, like the swifts that flash past, skimming in shrilly screaming groups over the lily pads.

The art of choosing just the right plant to achieve a certain desired effect while also creating the conditions for it to live a life of visible fulfilment is part of the virtuous cycle over which the gardener presides. Countess Marina Emo, the present owner, is consistently modest about the results she has achieved, for like any true gardener, she knows just how much of her success is due to luck, rather than design, and to the plants' volition rather than to her own persistence. She is particularly pleased with a wildflower meadow that has suddenly come into its own, for no reason she can think of except that she has been trying for years to encourage it. A purplish mist of wild clary (*Salvia verbenaca*) suspended above lush green grasses with a haze of copper beech in the background is

the unexpected reward. Beyond this, to the west, a wetland area has been created by allowing water from the perimeter ditch to form a shallow pond before leading it out again by means of a sluice gate that regulates the flow. Such ingenuity with the ways of water has been long in the making on this pan-flat plain where the marshlands are ever in abeyance. Herons, egrets and ducks are the birds most likely to be flying overhead, adding their croaking to the cacophony of frog calls.

The area behind the villa is divided roughly into four main areas, of which the largest, in the northwest corner, is the orchard with its rows of espaliered pear trees. It is bounded along its southern side by a magnificent avenue of *Magnolia grandiflora*. The cumulative effect of their robust, glossy foliage and their lusciously perfumed flowers in every stage of unfurling is of such overwhelming sensuality that it is almost a relief to emerge from the tunnel, as after a surfeit of exotic riches. In the central area, a large lawn surrounds the family coat of arms which

appears as a large slab of red and white stripes executed in gravel. Six acroterions play on the heraldic theme and the encircling privet hedge defines a symbolic as well as botanic boundary. The immobility and formality of this section is in contrast to the exuberant colours and shapes of the flowers massed in two long strips along either side of it. A herbaceous border is a rarity in Italy and the floral abundance of these long beds is quite startling. Again, much of the credit for the delightful associations of flower forms and shades that succeed each other from spring to autumn, is attributed to chance by its attentive gardener.

There is certainly more design than fortuitousness in the choice of a white banksia rose to clothe the little bower at the entrance to the hornbeam alley. The view from the curved stone table and chairs crosses the whole width of the garden to another bower, this one swathed in wisteria. But there is no continuation in the surrounding country-side, subjugated by a monoculture of sturdy maize. The startlingly conical shapes of the Euganean hills rise to the

north, west and south, and are present in the garden in the shape of the numerous woodland plants that populate the cheerful shade of the hornbeam alley enclosing three sides of the garden. They arrived here as 'snatchlings' from the neighbouring hills long before such acts were outlawed. The contessa likes to run her own little trials with shop-bought primroses and cyclamen in garish colours, watching gleefully as they rapidly revert to type and consort like natives with the anemones and sweet woodruff.

There is space for experiment here, but there is also the quiet restraint of an eye that recognises when nothing more needs adding. A *Rosa gigantea* that fans out over the front of a farmhouse annexe manages to be both elegant and rustic and the white geraniums on standby for the end of its flowering period will look similarly right in their plain pots spaced along the front. Large contrasting colour

LEFT It takes years of patient skill to produce an herbaceous border of such beauty in any climate, and that of the Po plain is particularly challenging.
ABOVE One of the fish ponds flanking the villa, its far bank lined with the feathery fronds of *Taxodium distichum*.
RIGHT Clumps of handsome flag irises have colonised the banks of the eastern fish pond.

'We think', she continues, her use of the first person plural conjuring the unlikely scenario of a Venetian secret society dedicated to matters horticultural,

> that an Englishwoman must have lived there once.
> How else would bluebells have got there? The place
> was neglected for years, yet they were still growing
> there when the garden was restored. For some reason
> – I wish I knew what it was – they found it amenable
> and have gone on flowering year after year ever since.

By means of such faint and fragile traces the gardener's actions are still discoverable, decades or even centuries after she has gone. That gardener may or may not have been English, may or may not have been a woman, but who it may have been is certainly intriguing, especially given the history of the occupancy of Palazzo Soranzo Cappello. Like ghostly footprints, the bluebells reappear each spring, giving rise to conjecture even in the shadow of the Euganean hills.

LEFT Late afternoon sunlight filters through a copper beech in an area of the garden planted as an arboretum.
BELOW Queen Anne's Lace. The great beauty of some of the commonest wild flowers is especially apparent in this garden.
RIGHT The wildflower meadow with its ox-eye daisies, buttercups and purple spikes of wild clary sage.

fields are preferred to mixtures and single botanical species are used to define each element of the garden so that their particular character may impose itself and create a distinct atmosphere. At the front of the villa, the rose beds which range from white through various shades of pink to deep red are justifiably famous. Another example of the success of this approach is in the verdant avenue of swamp cypress (*Taxodium distichum*) lining one side of the eastern fishpond: underplanted exclusively with *Iris japonica*, it is a place of peculiar freshness and lightness.

As we reach the end of the pergola, Countess Marina speaks of her longing to have more bluebells and bends to inspect a little drift of them growing on the margins of the hornbeam walk. 'I'll tell you a place that's strangely full of them, somewhere you'd never expect! And it's a bit of a mystery how they got there!' She is thinking of Palazzo Soranzo Cappello, in the courtyard of the Caesars.

ROVIGO

CA' DOLFIN-MARCHIORI

LENDINARA

ON 25 FEBRUARY 1867, ALMOST SIX YEARS after the Unification of Italy, Giuseppe Garibaldi stood on the balcony of Ca' Dolfin in the centre of Lendinara and made a short speech to the assembled crowds. On the balcony with the battle-scarred Hero of Two Worlds were some of his most trusted and devoted followers, all of whom had risked their lives in the cause of a free Italy. There was Alberto Mario, a native of Lendinara, and his wife, the English-born journalist Jessie White, both of whom had joined the Expedition of the Thousand in 1860 to free Sicily from Bourbon rule. There was Giovanni Acerbi, the first member of parliament for the newly established constituency of Lendinara, and then there was Domenico Marchiori, Garibaldi's host for the day and the first mayor of Lendinara. It must truly have seemed to those listeners, whose hearts were bursting with patriotic pride, that a new era had begun. From that day the street's name was changed from Via Nuova to Via Garibaldi.

Domenico Marchiori (1828–1905) was one of those worthy, energetic figures that the nineteenth century seems to have thrown up in great quantity. A highly educated man of many parts, from a distinguished and well-off family and with multiple artistic interests, Marchiori had lived in Lendinara since the age of twenty, after his father and uncle had bought the large sixteenth-century palazzo with its façade facing onto one of the town's most prestigious streets. Despite its modest dimensions, Lendinara had attained the title of city in 1495 and its centuries-old prosperity and industriousness were visible in its fine buildings, civic institutions and distinctive cultural life. The city's first printing press had been set up

The north façade of Ca' Dolfin-Marchiori. Elements of the *giardino all'italiana* live on in the careful symmetry of the garden adjacent to the orchard.

in 1695. Ca' Dolfin was built in the sixteenth century by a Venetian noble family with landed interests in the surrounding area, the fertile, flat and flood-prone plain known as the Polesine. The heat is relentless here in summer, the humidity debilitating and the rivers and open water channels breed mosquitoes in their millions. In winter, when the freezing fogs descend, there is isolation as the horizon disappears and everything familiar becomes muffled and indistinct. There are no woods, no hills, no summits, no sea. But the soil is capable of yielding great riches, and as Venice's maritime trade contracted and her nobles turned increasingly landwards in search of investment opportunities in the sixteenth century, the Polesine exerted great attraction, though more for the purposes of speculation than of *villeggiatura*.

Ca' Dolfin had a small garden space to the side of the house, with a high wall separating it from the street. Behind were fields, an orchard, vegetable garden and vineyard. Soon after moving in, Giovanni Marchiori bought adjoining pieces of land from a neighbouring convent and around 1860, he requested the deviation of water from the nearby Adigetto canal for irrigation purposes. His son Domenico, who had graduated in mathematics but whose true passion was poetry and painting, had time on his hands now that the main political issue of the Italian century had been settled. Towards 1870 he conceived the idea of transforming the garden around Ca' Dolfin into a garden dedicated to poetry, in which he could indulge his love for storytelling and treat his friends to long afternoons of play-acting and fantasy. He began by converting the small house on the edge of the small garden, facing, like the palazzo, onto the street, in order to provide a separate entrance to his creation. Its neo-gothic appearance transported guests back in time and place so that as soon as they stepped past the threshold the adventure could begin.

A series of themed grottoes followed, connected by dark, winding corridors designed to disorient and heighten the sense of drama. After reconversion into the custodian's house, only the shell grotto survives of this complex. The pearly insides of the remaining shells with which the walls are encrusted still gleam faintly in the blueish-green submarine light cast by tinted glass panels high up on the domed ceiling. Stone benches around the walls suggest that guests might have been invited to sit down as they were regaled with stories about the brigands, magicians and hermits who had once, or perhaps still, inhabited the grottoes. From here they were conducted into a dark wood full of the sound of rushing water where, along a meandering path shaded by pine, yew and box and brushing past the variegated leaves of aucuba, they could discover various scenes designed to surprise and delight them and to evoke feelings of nostalgia for lost worlds. Artful compositions of carefully chosen plants and simulated architectures prompted indefinable emotions of yearning for what had never been and could never be,

LEFT Under the dense canopy of leaves, a greenish pall lies over the stone busts that merge with tree roots by a small footbridge.

from a covered bridge, the interior of which was painted with Japanese scenes. Events were arranged in such a way that some guests were left behind to wave to the occupants of the boat as it passed beneath them into a dark tunnel. This passageway has now silted up so it is no longer possible to float through and emerge, as intended, onto the wide curve of the lake on the other side, where sunlight danced off the surface of the water and lit the pensive forms of a statue placed like a figurehead on the tip of a little island. One imagines that here, under the deep shade and heady perfumes of the magnolias, the garden reached its poetic climax – literally if the small amphitheatre of dishevelled white stones was used, as it would appear, for the recitation of verse. But the little audience of passengers was only momentarily set down on the island's shores, however, for this was by no means the end of their journey; Marchiori had one more surprise in store.

but sometimes might just be glimpsed, existing in the shaft of light penetrating a glade in which Roman sculptures lay scattered on the mossy ground, or in a lofty gothic archway ennobled with heraldic insignia.

The fisherman's hut still stands, straddling a rushing stream that courses over rocks just in front of its rustic balcony. A stage-managed torrent is an impressive artifice in a place where water is only ever still or slow moving, channelled and deflected into the grid of straight lines that cut up the vast, unending plain. In Marchiori's garden there is the illusion of water behaving as if in the wild; it splashes, tumbles, seethes and is then suddenly slowed at a bend where stone steps lead down to the water's edge. The remains of the Chinese pagoda that once concealed a landing stage still stand in a tangle of undergrowth, its fragile structure of tinted metal sheeting no match for the encroaching wood. Here guests could board a rowing boat and, slipping the mooring rope, be transported on water for the rest of their tour around the garden. The beginning of their journey could be witnessed from across the river

ABOVE Along the banks of a bubbling stream, cast concrete imitates rustic wooden fence poles and has attracted a thick coat of moss.
RIGHT The covered bridge, with its oval doorway and fragments of a Japanese-inspired painted interior.

The old city walls of Lendinara had been demolished towards the end of the sixteenth century, but here and there traces of their massive ramparts remained, and one such indelible mound of building rubble was to be found right inside the Marchiori's newly enlarged property, at its western end. It was an ideal place to carve out an icehouse and this was duly done, but the potential for something more was inherent in a pile of rubble of this size and Marchiori could not resist. A medieval tower was erected on top of it, towering over the tops of the surrounding trees, complete with pinnacles and an internal winding staircase leading up to a belvedere with incomparable views of the whole garden. This far corner of the property could be reached by rowing through bright pools of water

BELOW The gothic archway of brick with terracotta decorations, marking the boundary of the small area in which the first part of the narrative takes place. RIGHT Antique columns and the spotted leaves of *Aucuba japonica*: an unmistakably nineteenth-century association.

that alternated with murky, shadowy areas under overhanging boughs and then along a canal covered over by the airy light green of a hornbeam avenue. Originally the river encircled the mound completely like a moat and guests could finally disembark at a gate in the boundary wall at the top of Via Garibaldi, where a carriage awaited to conduct them back to the house. Perhaps, if the day were still fine, they would have been led through the atrium and out again to partake of refreshments in the neat and secluded garden by the side of the house. This was reached by way of an anteroom decorated by Marchiori with paintings of watery, fantastical landscapes framed by trompe l'oeil crumbling brickwork, gothic tracery and fronds of greenery. And so the visit would come to an end, amidst laughter and recollection and gratitude for a few hours of pleasant escapism. Only the tinkling fountain with its sinister goat-faced dolphin, clam shells and tortoise might have called to mind the strange adventure that had just taken place in the innocent-looking *boschetto* that bordered one side of this secret garden.

ABOVE The northern approach to the villa is separated from the garden by a canal. The solution is this bridge with benches suspended over the water.

In the years that followed, Marchiori was elected as a member of parliament, but he was not an enthusiastic politician, preferring to stay on home ground where he oversaw the building of new roads, was instrumental in the creation of a rail link connecting Lendinara to Rovigo and Legnago, instituted a technical school at which he himself taught French, and built the first sugar-processing plant in the area. Disease and poverty continued, however, to be the lot of the landless peasantry whose subsistence diet of polenta produced from the maize that grew so well on the plains of the Polesine made them prone to pellagra, a life-threatening condition that formed a deadly triad with the already endemic malaria and typhoid. In the last two decades of the century thousands emigrated to South America in search of a better life.

Marchiori's poems were published posthumously by his children in a small volume illustrated with photographs of the garden in its heyday, a precious reminder of an epoch that seems strangely distant in time, further even than that evoked by the area to the north of Ca' Dolfin-Marchiori's sober, sixteenth-century façade, with its regular, symmetrical planting, cones of clipped yew and the reassuring presence of lemon trees and tender varieties of jasmine in terracotta pots.

TREVISO

VILLA BARBARO
MASER

IT MAY SEEM AT FIRST SIGHT THAT VILLA Barbaro, glowing ochre and cream against its dark backdrop of wooded hills, has no garden to offer. After all, there are very few ornamental plants or trees, no shady paths or leafy avenues inviting the visitor to explore the wide green skirts of lawn spread out before it. What planting there was has long since disappeared and no documentary evidence exists to enlighten us as to the garden's original appearance. Today it is stripped down to its bare essentials in an uncompromisingly geometric alternation of gravel paths, stone and lawn in which, however, are recognisable the core elements of Palladian architecture: symmetry, harmony and proportion. A garden does exist here, as will be seen, though not in the ordinary sense of a collection of plants. This is a garden of architecture, in which proportion and space provide the conditions for water, painting and sculpture to express a unique sense of place.

A Venetian noble family of some distinction, the Barbaro had produced eminent scholars, statesmen and bishops in the fifteenth century, notably Ermolao the Younger (1454–93) who made important contributions to Renaissance humanist thought with his translations and commentaries of Aristotle. His descendants, the brothers Daniele (1513–70) and Marcantonio (1518–95), were also highly educated men who, while carving out very different careers, collaborated closely on the rebuilding of the family villa on their lands at Maser in the hills near Asolo, north-east of Venice. Following his studies in mathematics, philosophy and astronomy at the University of Padua, Daniele had worked with the physician Pietro da Noale on the organisation and design of the Orto Botanico

instituted there in 1545 (see pages 76–83). His initial plans for this richly symbolical garden of simples included many elements of Roman inspiration, revealing an early interest in the architecture of antiquity. Shortly after this he began the monumental work of translating the Roman architect Vitruvius's *De Architectura*, which was eventually published in a critical edition with notes in 1556. Daniele was both a diplomat, serving as Venetian ambassador to the English court between 1549 and 1551 and Patriarch-elect of Aquilea, but architecture was his abiding passion and during the decade 1550–60 he consulted frequently with the architect Andrea Palladio, who provided most of the illustrations of ancient buildings for the Vitruvius translation.

Born Andrea della Gondola, the son of a stonemason from Padua, Palladio had been taken under the wing of the humanist poet and scholar Gian Giorgio Trissino

LEFT A statue of Neptune faces the villa, ready to receive its outflow of water and direct it to the fields at his back.
RIGHT The remains of two fountains are still visible in the centre of the regularly spaced lawns in front of the villa.

(1478–1550) while at work on the latter's villa at Cricoli near Vicenza. Trissino renamed his protégé Palladio, it is said, after Pallas Athena, the Greek goddess identified by the Romans as Minerva, goddess of wisdom, and encouraged him in the study of architecture. This, in the intellectual circles in which Trissino moved, meant ancient Roman architecture, both as it was theorised in the works of Vitruvius and of his modern interpreters Sebastiano Serlio (1475–1554) and Leon Battista Alberti (1404–72), and as practised by contemporary Roman architects such as Bramante (1444–1515). Above all, it entailed observation at first hand of antique buildings, and during the 1540s Palladio accompanied Trissino to Rome on several occasions. In 1554 he again undertook a study trip there,

BELOW Set amidst vineyards and fields of maize, the agricultural context of Palladio's 'casa di villa' is intact.

ABOVE On the tympanum, Spartan heroes are saved by love (dolphins) and united by peace (the bull) under the protection of concord (the eagle).
RIGHT The barchesse or farm buildings extend out on either side of the villa's central body, surmounted by dovecots with sundials.

this time in the company of Daniele Barbaro, and it was on their return from this journey in 1554 that Daniele, together with his brother, commissioned Palladio to restructure and enlarge their existing villa at Maser.

During the sixteenth century improvements and investments in the land became the state policy of the Serenissima, as it attempted to become self-sufficient in grain and other commodities previously imported from its eastern empire. The Venetian aristocracy began to spend increasingly long periods of time on their newly purchased or enlarged estates, overseeing the running of their affairs. Consequently, there was an increasing demand for residences that were both functional in design and noble in appearance and could offer civilised living conditions and efficient use of space for all the equipment and storage necessary for large-scale estates. What was singular in Palladio's approach was his organisation of the villa and farm buildings into a single, unified whole. The results were grandiose yet intensely practical in purpose, and not the least of their appeal – especially to the modest gentry who made up most of Palladio's clientele – resided in the fact that they were built of relatively inexpensive brick and stucco. Palladio conferred a classical dignity to the business of farm management with his temple-inspired façades, giving a sacred aura to the client's presence on the land, and to his business and leisure pursuits. Beneath the elegance was a rational core.

At Villa Barbaro there are indications that the commission was not altogether easy to expedite, for the Barbaro brothers had their own very precise ideas about what they wanted and the expertise to put it into practice. Architectural historians point to several incongruities in the villa's design. Despite pursuing a high-profile political career, Marcantonio also liked to dabble in architecture and was a prolific amateur sculptor. At Villa Barbaro he had no qualms about placing his handiwork next to that of Alessandro Vittoria (1525–1608), one of the leading sculptors in the Veneto. The result of this three-way collaboration is in many ways an atypical Palladian villa, although its basic layout is similar to Villa Emo at Fanzolo, consisting as it does of a central body flanked by two low, colonnaded *barchesse* linking it to the dovecots on either side. As the hub of a large agricultural estate, these long outbuildings contained the stables, barns, bakehouses,

wine cellars and other rooms necessary for the storage and transformation of agricultural products.

When Palladio came to write his own architectural treatise, *The Four Books of Architecture*, he specified that a villa should be sited at the centre of the property and that it should be raised, isolating it from the surrounding country, both in order to enjoy the views and in order to endow it with an appropriate dignity and pre-eminence which would in turn reflect the status of the owners. The fact that at Maser he was building on top of a pre-existing building explains why both site and position diverged considerably from the ideal in this case, for Villa Barbaro is nestled into the foot of a hillside with a gently rising slope of land in front of it. It is neither isolated nor central,

In the secret garden behind the villa, a grotto set into the hillside forms the centrepiece of the elegant nymphaeum.

being set on the margins of the property. But one important prerequisite was present in the form of a readily available supply of water from a spring arising in the woods behind the villa. This, according to the architect who recommended that villas be always sited next to a river or a spring, was vital both to the agricultural premise of the villa and to the good health of the occupants. It was also central to the idea of a garden.

In his account of Villa Barbaro, Palladio gave a detailed description of the complex itinerary of this precious resource and how he used it to link the various parts of the villa complex. Captured at source in a collecting tank above the house, it flowed into the grotto that is the central element of the nymphaeum and then out into the semi-circular fish pond, around which are ranged statues in niches. The water then entered the villa's kitchens and passed out again into various fountains and ponds in front of the villa where, after irrigating the garden on both sides of its central axis, it flowed down to the public road. Here

it once filled two water troughs for animals, before being channelled underground to emerge in the fountain of Neptune on the other side. Finally, it was used to irrigate the orchard beyond, a *brolo* described by Palladio as being 'very large and full of superb fruit and various wild plants'. Something akin to this blend of the functional and the ornamental, albeit in an urban context, would have been visible to Daniele Barbaro and Palladio in 1554 in the newly completed Villa Giulia in Rome, which included a nymphaeum designed by Bartolomeo Ammannati (1511–92). Giorgio Vasari, the chronicler of Renaissance artists and architects, was one of the first to comment on the similarities between the two complexes in the 1568 edition of his *Vite degli Artisti*. This visit also coincided with the planning stages of the spectacular garden and villa at Tivoli, designed by Pirro Ligorio (1513–83) for Cardinal Ippolito d'Este, which contained extensive water features. Barbaro dedicated his edition of Vitruvius to the cardinal, and Palladio is known to have exchanged drawings of antique buildings with Ligorio.

The garden may thus be said to originate with the entrance of water into the grotto that forms the

Unfortunately the original spring can no longer be relied upon to keep the pool filled throughout the year, nor does it any longer pour from the amphora held by the river god into the bath below or from the various orifices of the encircling deities. It does, however, spurt abundantly from the breasts of a figure on the highest point of the pediment above. From this point on, the iconographical programme that links statuary and painted decoration, both inside and outside the villa, is intertwined with water in a sophisticated narrative that is in all probability owed to the erudite Daniele Barbaro. The ten Greek divinities in the niches of the nymphaeum hemicycle are all custodians of woodland and water, and their meanings are further elucidated by poetic epigrams in Italian. Four telamons, two old and two young male figures of colossal proportions, thought to be the work of Marcantonio Barbaro, hold up the base of the richly decorated pediment (which bears symbols of Love and Responsibility, virtues found also on the façade of the villa).

ABOVE Of the nymphaeum's once numerous water tricks, only this female statue still obliges (with a little help from behind the scenes).
RIGHT AND FAR RIGHT The two bearded telamons at the furthermost ends of the nymphaeum. The stucco sculptures and richly ornamented friezes seem to have been the result of a collaboration between Alessandro Vittoria and his patron, Marcantonio Barbaro.

centrepiece of the nymphaeum. Visible just outside the glass doors to the rear of the central atrium of the *piano nobile*, the nymphaeum with its semicircular fish pond encloses the north side of a rectangular court behind the villa. An elliptical structure ornately decorated with stucco statuary and reliefs of festoons of flowers and fruit held up by putti in half-relief, it appears as a mediating barrier between the unruly natural forces of the woodland behind and the civilised and harmoniously organised spaces of the villa's garden in front. In the dark recess under the central arch, dug out of the hill, a river god reclines in a pumice-stone niche, a primordial setting that contrasts utterly with the sophistication of the fresco decoration by Paolo Veronese in the barrel vault above, centred on the theme of Peace and Abundance.

VOLTI DI DONNE DELICATI E BELLI

VOMINI ACCORTI E TRATTI A GENTILEZZA

MASTRI IN ARME, IN DESTRIERI ED IN VCCELLI

Inside the villa, real and invented space intermingles in Veronese's witty and dazzlingly illusionistic frescoes in which the patron's family, servants, pets, and even the painter himself appear as spectators to scenes from Olympus that centre around the concepts of universal harmony and divine love. Mythological, astrological and religious themes are interwoven in such a way as to reinforce the message that through peace and concord in men's affairs, from conjugal love, the creation of a family, the tilling of the fields, and the governing of the state, universal harmony may be achieved. Here and there amidst the deities, allegorical figures and the personifications of virtues are trellises bearing foliage and fruits outlined against patches of bright blue sky. Elsewhere the paintings seem to perforate the walls, like windows opening out onto fantastical seascapes and cityscapes, or landscapes with villas or ancient ruins. In one of these Villa Barbaro itself appears.

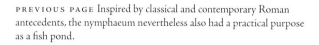

PREVIOUS PAGE Inspired by classical and contemporary Roman antecedents, the nymphaeum nevertheless also had a practical purpose as a fish pond.

ABOVE TOP A *trompe l'oeil* vine trellis in the villa extends it to the fields outside and celebrates the fecundity of the villa-farm.
ABOVE Vines and nectarine-like fruits are tied by *stroppe*, or lengths of willow branch, a method still in use today.

From the front window of the *piano nobile* is a view across the quadrangular terrace below and down along the central axis that divides the grassy slope in front of the villa. Eight ponds and fountains were once disposed in the evenly spaced squares that descend towards the road. Statues emphasise the junctures of a wide hemicycle that divides the smaller, more intimate spaces near the villa from the larger meadows below. Beyond the low wall that separates the property from the road, a second hemicycle continues the design. Neptune, accompanied by Time and Fortune, stands elevated on a clamshell, waiting to receive the waters and direct them finally to the fields behind him.

At his back, the axis continues through high wrought-iron gates, along an avenue of limes that proceeds across the land to infinity.

In 1580 Marcantonio Barbaro commissioned Palladio to design a small parish church and family chapel at the entrance to the neighbouring village of Cornuda. The *tempietto* that resulted took its inspiration from the Roman pantheon and was Palladio's last task. He died in August of that year.

From the windows of the first floor, the Barbaro brothers could survey their lands, stretching into the plain along an avenue of limes.

VERONA

VILLA DELLA TORRE

FUMANE

ALMOST HALF A MILLENNIUM HAS PASSED since Giulio Della Torre built his mannerist version of a Roman villa on a hillside outside the village of Fumane in the Valpolicella region north of Verona. Centuries of rain and wind have scoured its roofs while lichen and mosses have crept over its mottled grey stones and the sun faded its ochre stucco. An air of permanence has settled over its ancient walls and broad descending terraces, as if they had become one with the vine-covered slopes and gently enfolding contours of the surrounding landscape. No matter that in the present day Villa Della Torre earns its living as the headquarters of a renowned wine producer and is at the hub of its myriad business activities – the solidity and apparent sobriety of its layout reassures and satisfies, not least because it alludes to the very earliest origins of the western European concept of garden.

The decision to enlarge a pre-existing villa by building another one alongside and organising the living spaces around a peristyle was anachronistic for the mid-sixteenth

LEFT Giulio Della Torre's country villa was built for the enjoyment of leisurely *otium*, far from the cares of *negotium* in the city.

ABOVE The peristyle looking northwest. The columns are built with varying numbers of stone blocks.

century and certainly ran counter to the ideas of contemporaries such as Palladio who, from the 1540s onwards, had been developing a type of temple-fronted country villa for his landed patrons in which house and agricultural annexes were ennobled alike, in a single, unified building that expressed magnificence through the harmonic use of classical forms but without ever losing sight of the practical purposes for which it was intended. A comparison of Villa Della Torre, which seems to have been completed around 1558, with the almost contemporary Villa Barbaro at Maser shows how far apart these two conceptions were (see pages 131–39). Villa Della Torre's agricultural buildings are tucked out of sight beyond the southwest perimeter wall. Yet the architects of both based their designs on the rediscovery of the antique, and specifically on the architectural writings and surviving buildings of classical Rome.

The house and lands of Fumane were part of the rich dowry bestowed upon Anna Maffei upon her marriage in 1504 to Giulio Della Torre. The Della Torre was an aristocratic and learned Veronese family, with political and ecclesiastical connections throughout the Veneto, and though Giulio followed a distinguished career in law he was in many ways a typical Renaissance man, pursuing many diverse interests. He was a passionate antiquarian and a collector of bronze medals, many of which he cast himself. Although the names of Giulio Romano or Michele Sanmichele have in the past been proposed as the possible architects of Villa Della Torre, it is now thought more likely that to a significant extent the villa's conception is owed to Giulio Della Torre himself, who planned it as a *locus amoenus* in which his wide circle of erudite friends could come together in pleasurable and stimulating surroundings to talk, to exchange ideas, read poetry and philosophise far into the night. More recently, scholars have noted some intriguing correspondences with the theoretical works of Sebastiano Serlio (1475–c.1554), but whoever was responsible for the magnificent complex, their brief was to provide a residence for the practice of *otium* rather than *negotium*, according to the distinction

made by ancient Roman writers between leisure and business. It was to be a place of rural retirement, offering the possibility of restoring both mind and body by means of pleasurable physical and mental pursuits. Work on the villa was probably begun after 1535 – the wars resulting from the League of Cambrai between 1508 and 1516 had devastated the countryside and recovery was slow – and completed by around 1560.

The peristyle arrangement would have been known to Della Torre through the earliest surviving treatise on architecture, *The Ten Books of Architecture* by the Roman architect and engineer Vitruvius (80–25 BC). The first printed copies of this work were issued in Rome in 1486 and were enthusiastically read by scholars during that

LEFT The view to the southeast, showing the terrace overlooking the lower garden beyond. Villa and garden are laid out over five levels.
RIGHT Brick shows through the crumbling stucco that imitates monumental stone blocks on this entrance gate.

period of resurgent interest in Greek and Roman culture and rebirth of learning that we call the Renaissance. Palladio himself provided the drawings for the first translation into Italian of this fundamental work by his patron Daniele Barbaro, owner of Villa Barbaro at Maser. Vitruvius had pointed out the importance of spacious peristyles in the Greek manner, and had helpfully provided precise indications as to their proportions. The predecessors of the monastic cloister, these colonnaded courtyards of Greco–Roman tradition provided at once an outdoor room in which to receive large numbers of people and a covered walkway in which to perambulate when the weather was inclement. At Villa Della Torre it was decorated with statues in niches from which water tumbled into basins below, adding to the plashing of water in the central fountain and the gurgling rivulets emanating from grotesque masks affixed to the four central columns. The air would have been full of the wafting perfumes of flowering plants and shrubs in pots. As in the *domus antiqua* of Ancient Rome the *peristylum* would have formed the very heart of the house, the most important part of the whole building. Walks in the open air, instead, could be taken on the broad raised walkways that skirt the northwest side of the villa, forming an *ambulatorium* beneath its high enclosing walls that was protected from the north winds.

This is the first part of the complex now seen by visitors turning into the entrance gate from the road that continues along the former *brolo*, or orchard, above the villa, but originally the entrance was situated below, and the approach to the villa, which faces southeast across gently rolling countryside, was through a wooded area full of cypresses and other evergreens, traversed by canals and dotted with fountains, amongst which flowers bloomed and trees bore fruits in every season. This, at least, is how it was described by the famous Venetian courtesan and poetess Veronica Franco (1546–91) who dedicated to her host Marcantonio Della Torre a long poem in praise of Fumane, which she published in her volume *Terze Rime*

LEFT The peristyle looking northwest towards the outer gate and the vineyards. The original, and larger, stone basin is now in the garden.
RIGHT The octagonal *tempietto* and its bell tower, which Vasari attributed to the Veronese architect Michele Sanmichele (1484–1559).

in 1575. In part a conventional exercise in courtly deference and in part, we might imagine, a genuinely moved response to the sights and sounds of the countryside and the fecundity of the gardens – for the author was a creature of the drawing rooms, the narrow *calli* and the confined spaces of her native city – Franco's verses return again and again to the richness and variety of the lands in Della Torre's possession and the rural delights to be experienced therein:

> The lovely garden's appearance gives pleasure,
> and as you admire the elegance there
> of every well-kept and neatly planted part,
>   you see hares and rabbits, darting swiftly and boldly;
> and while you regret that such a scene
> did not sooner catch your eye,

now from another side come forth
roaming herds of deer, goats, buck, and other game,
which increase your wonder and delight.
    But then among these animals in herds
you see, set apart from the garden,
the water meadow with narrow, clear canals,
    and you see, in the far-off waves, the shimmer
of darting fish, which seem to be silver
as they swim from side to side.

This large, walled area below the villa, a hunting enclosure stocked with game which Veronica Franco loved to look upon from above, resting her arm on the marble balustrade as she watched birds, beasts and fish being netted, limed, trapped and caught, is presently an expanse of rough grass threaded through with tough little wild

plants like the peppery-scented lesser calamint that thrives in arid pastures. The large pool with fountain that once formed its centrepiece, and which appears in a map of 1752, lasted until the Second World War when it was demolished.

In her paean to the bounty of nature, Franco omitted to mention one of the more striking aspects of the villa's garden. Directly below the double ramp of steps leading up to the raised terrace in front of the villa, a remarkable sight greets the eye in the form of an anthropomorphic face fashioned roughly out of boulders of travertine and quartz. The gaping mouth is a doorway giving onto a small, vaulted chamber with a central, octagonal pilaster that conceals a monstrous sculpted mask set into the back wall. Water from the fish pond above gushed out from this orifice, crossed the chamber and was channelled into the

gardens. Together with the grotto-nymphaeum of Villa Barbaro and the long-lost example of the same at Palazzo Trevisan on the island of Murano in Venice, this grotto is among the first of its kind in the Veneto. Traces of the river pebbles and stalactites embedded in its walls remain, together with the pearly translucencies of shells and rose quartz that would have flickered and glittered in the leaping flames of braziers or torches lit in the dark interconnecting alcoves spaced around the sides.

The polymath humanist and architectural theorist Leon Battista Alberti (1404–72) had been the first to recommend the re-introduction of grottoes or *nymphaea* as garden elements in his influential architectural treatise *De Re Aedificatoria* of 1483. The Villa Della Torre grotto seems to follow his advice to the letter, though inspiration may also have come from the slightly earlier Hell's Mouth in the Sacro Bosco, the bizarre mannerist garden at Bomarzo in construction from 1552. Meanwhile, excavations of Hadrian's Villa at Tivoli, which contained a grotto of Hades, were ongoing, arousing great interest in humanist

LEFT A flight of semicircular stone steps links the lawns at the back of the villa with the perimeter walkway, planted with olive trees.
ABOVE Vineyards cover the sloping land above Villa Della Torre in what was formerly a walled *brolo*.

and artistic circles. Bramante and Raphael visited the site in the first years of the century, but it was only in the mid-century with the archaeological work of the architect Pirro Ligorio (1513–83) that it was systematically described.

The grotto may have been the guest's first introduction to one of the themes of the villa-garden complex: metamorphosis. The allusions to a subterranean, irrational world simmering just below the surface patina of civilisation were continued in the villa in the series of spectacular fireplaces in the form of grotesque masks, sculpted by Bartolommeo Ridolfi (died before 1570) which adorn four of the rooms on the ground floor. The walls, according to Franco, were decorated with stories from Ovid's *Metamorphoses*, in which the various permutations of Jupiter's transfiguring power and his deceptions of various innocents such as Io, Europa, Danaë, Ganymede and Callisto would have given ample scope for erotic and sensual explorations of the themes of transformation.

Another sign that everything was not what it seemed was in the peristyle itself. The expectation of a harmonious symmetry, reinforced by the axial perspective that runs through the villa from the monumental gate at its rear, through its centre and out again to the far end of the bottom terrace, is shaken by the appearance of the peristyle's encircling columns which are instead fashioned from crudely hewn and irregularly-sized blocks of stone. It is as if a rude, amorphous energy is erupting, capable of distorting and disturbing the built space, and of upsetting the carefully measured proportions of the known world. Yet here, in all probability, was also where the perfumed orange and citron trees grew neatly in their terracotta pots, as sure a sight of reassuring loveliness as could be conjured in a mannerist garden.

But the outstanding feature of Villa Della Torre was the great abundance of fresh spring water channelled from up country which vivified the atmosphere with its sound and its light-catching movement. Gravity and narrow pipes produced sufficient pressure for spurting jets in the fountains and tap water in the rooms, after which the water flowed (and still flows) copiously into the fish pond, given pride of place outside the villa's front door and of such dimensions that it needed a triple-arched bridge to span it. From here it descended to the grotto below and finally ran into the 'lovely field', 'adorned with rare trees and a mantle ever green'. The novelty and pleasure of fresh running water is evident in Veronica Franco's poem where it is described as seemingly longing to follow close behind the master of the house, to wash his hands and do his bidding, after which:

> From this water a fountain is formed,
> which pours forth pure silver everywhere
> from a fast-running, fresh stream of crystal.
> Into the fertile land heaven instills
> a power that brings forth sweet fruit
> and makes the air healthful and serene;

A remarkable survivor, the villa and its grounds were in a ruinous state at the end of the Second World War, having been used as a garrison and as shelter for displaced civilians. It was later restored by the Cazzola family and is now surrounded by vineyards heavy with purple grapes used in the making of the Amarone wine for which the Cantina Allegrini, the present owners, are famed.

LEFT The arched bridge of Roman appearance that crosses the large fish pond and leads onto the upper terrace.
RIGHT Soot blackens the maw of one of the still-used fireplaces in a reception room at Villa Della Torre.

GIARDINO GIUSTI

IN A DINGY AND UNREMARKABLE STREET IN the northeast of Verona, a large brown door stands open, inviting us to peer into the penumbra of an inner courtyard. Beyond it, across a pool of light and framed by rusticated gateposts embellished with obelisks, is a spectacular and justly celebrated vista. On the other side of ornate wrought-iron gates, towering cypresses line a narrow avenue that recedes far into the distance then ascends towards the pitch black of a cavernous arch dug out of what appears to be a rock bluff. Directly above, suspended at a dizzying height and fringed by vegetation, is a monstrous face with lips curled back to reveal pointed teeth. 'For pure sensation', commented the antiquarian and garden writer Sir George Sitwell, 'there is nothing in Italy equal to this first glimpse through the Giusti gateway.' Many of the visitors who have been privileged to walk around the garden since the Giusti family first opened it to the public five centuries ago would probably concur.

This enduring capacity to surprise is owed to a deliberate theatricality in the garden's conception and to the use of perspectival tricks that maximise the dramatic potential of its unusual and spectacular site. The courtyard between palazzo and garden is grandiose in its lofty simplicity, a presage of the great and complex riches to come. Brick battlements decorate the ivy-clad wall that separates it from the garden and on either side of the central gateway are wall fountains surmounted by niches containing statues of Apollo and Athena. There is birdsong and the sound of trickling water, the cooling breath of a lushly

verdant expanse sensed just beyond the wall, a hush as if we were on the verge of something.

The city quickly fades as we enter by one of the two side gates and the major themes present themselves. A swirling proliferation of box parterre weaves patterns over the ground, here enclosing a lawn, there a fountain. It then slopes gently up to a thicket of trees, which, as we will realise only later as we ascend the path winding through it in the deep shade of ilex and yew, conceals a steep cliff. Running across the length and breadth of the space like vertical waves of dark green velvet, marshalling and

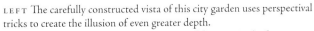

LEFT The carefully constructed vista of this city garden uses perspectival tricks to create the illusion of even greater depth.
RIGHT Apollo surmounts an antique-inspired fountain in the forecourt. The garden still contains many of Agostino Giusti's Roman inscriptions.

ordering our vision by turns, are tall cypresses, some of which, like the hoary old specimen at the entrance known as 'Goethe's Cypress', are of inestimable age. Below, the shiny leaves of lemon trees, raised on stone plinths in elegant terracotta pots, reflect glints of yellow sunlight. Then there is water, its steady quenching flow brimming over the rims of two moss-covered basins into shallow pools beneath. We stop to contemplate the statuary, the creamy forms of gesticulating deities: Diana, Apollo, Adonis, Juno, Venus, frozen in some inscrutable movement that evinces their eternal drama.

The Giusti name has been associated with this plot of land since medieval times, when they plied their trade as wool dyers. The family fortunes grew apace, as did their scholarly leanings. In 1565, Pier Francesco Giusti, a man of refinement and culture and a collector of antiquities,

assigned part of his magnificent new Renaissance palace to the city's Accademia Filarmonica. Although primarily dedicated to music, the academy's participation in the new ideals of humanism that were invigorating all branches of learning and the arts, made it a hub for the intellectual elite of Verona. It was in such a cultural milieu that Pier Francesco's music-loving son, Agostino Giusti (1546–1615) grew up, and it is mainly to him that the creation of that most sensual and intellectual artefact possessed by the Renaissance gentleman – a garden of delight – is attributed.

The garden's changing appearance over the centuries is richly documented, since it has been a famous (and accessible) landmark from its inception. Early descriptions make it clear that originally the garden was intended to shock and surprise its visitors, offering a dramatic itinerary that knowingly played on the emotions. One such account, a florid dialogue by Francesco Pona entitled *Sileno* published in Verona in 1620, is fascinating as much for the evidence of what has subsequently disappeared as for the descriptions of structures that are still extant. Pona describes lawns bordered by rose hedges, said to be so dappled with coloured flowers as to rival the very heavens in their variety and beauty. Beyond, a path led up through a shady laurel grove consecrated to the Muses, at the end of which was a place denominated the 'Kingdom of flowers', where visitors were amazed to discover plants flowering in all seasons, together with an abundance of lemons, oranges and citrons, as well as perfumed jasmine.

There is a valuable description of the garden's focal point, the now almost empty grotto, which vividly communicates the sense of awe and consternation felt by the seventeenth-century visitor as he came face to face with his own reflection and that of the garden behind him in mirrors of unprecedented size placed on the back wall. The otherworldly effect of this primordial den excavated from the bare cliff face was heightened by such 'sweet horrors' as stalactites, corals, shells and mother of pearl. Painted landscapes in niches completed the illusion while a tangible sense of reality was provided by a fountain and water tricks supplied by a cistern in the upper garden.

LEFT The garden's *genius loci*, Bacchus, Roman god of wine, once stood in the lemon house along the west wall. His goblet was lost to thieves.
RIGHT The subtleties of reposeful green have replaced the brilliantly coloured carpets of flowers of the early Giardino Giusti which 'rivalled those of Persia'.

The grotto was a must-have feature of gardens of this time, but this one evidently surpassed expectations. When the English traveller Thomas Coryat saw it in 1608, he was reminded of the garden of Sir Francis Carew of Middlesex, in which he had seen, 'one most excellent rocke there framed all by arte, and beautified with many elegant conceits, notwithstanding it is somewhat inferiour unto this'.

Many built elements noted by Pona are still recognisable today: the arcaded loggia in pink Verona stone halfway up the cliff at the western end of the garden still offers distant views over the rooftops of Verona, while the tower built against the cliff face and encasing a spiral stone staircase continues to provide the only access to the highest point of the garden. As one ascends this tower, an opening into the cliff allows a glimpse of the family chapel set in its deep recess, while on the other side, a series of windows afford increasingly giddy views of the garden below. At the top is a hillocky strip of land where vines, artichokes and herbs were once grown and where a curved balustrade forms a belvedere directly above the main cypress avenue. Pona makes no mention of the grotesque mask below this, from which flames could be made to leap, other than to remark that the garden's natural and artificial scenography was exploited to the full during the lively musical renditions of episodes from the lives of the gods, penned by erudite members of the Accademia Filarmonica themselves.

No better setting could have been provided for the third performance of Torquato Tasso's dramatised narrative *Aminta*, given here, complete with musical accompaniment, on 1 May 1581. Tragically, its author could not be present since he was in prison, having suffered what might now be termed a nervous breakdown. Written for the court of the Duke of Ferrara in 1573, it is a pastoral tale of a shepherd's unrequited love for a nymph, set in a bucolic world of rivers, fountains and woods, in which the tranquil order of the Golden Age is upset by the ambivalent and violent force of love. The plot of *Aminta* may almost be read as a metaphor for the complex and multi-layered meanings of this enigmatic garden, in which a subtle

---

Apollo is represented in his role as patron of poetry and music. Behind him, the once bare rock bluff is concealed by 'English-style' woodland.

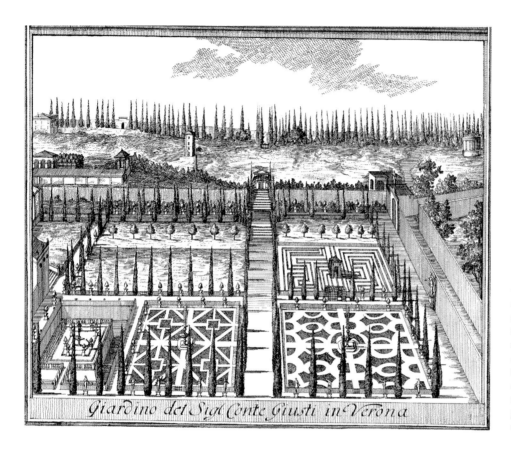

Giardino del Sigᵗ Conte Giusti in Verona

LEFT The Giusti Garden's citrus collection qualified it for inclusion in J. C. Volkamer's *Continuation der Nürnbergischen Hesperidum* of 1714.

ABOVE RIGHT The giddy view south towards the city centre from the belvedere above the stone mask, at the highest point of the garden.

RIGHT A line of young cypresses crosses the garden from east to west, part of a restoration scheme to reinstate the sixteenth-century layout.

tension exists between the initial impression of quiet harmony and the undercurrent of untamed and archaic impulses that gradually suggest themselves.

A detailed engraving made by the German botanist Johann Christoph Volkamer shows that in 1714, the southeast section of the lower garden included a large, rectangular fish pond bounded by a balustrade and with an island at its centre on which a statue of Venus stood, recalling that of Villa Lante di Bagnaia. This was filled in as part of the nineteenth-century Romantic relandscaping undertaken by the Veronese architect Luigi Trezza (see Giardino di Pojega, Villa Rizzardi, pages 170–77) and replaced, as were the stiffly geometrical Renaissance patterns of the front two sections of the garden, with the more rounded, swirling parterre forms in the French style that have survived to the present day. The statues around which the parterres are organised were sculpted by Lorenzo Muttoni in the mid-eighteenth century. Trezza also removed the row of cypresses that crossed the middle of the garden from east to west, in order to create a fashionably sweeping vista, but these have now been replanted in an attempt to partially restore the garden's sixteenth-century layout.

Volkamer's engraving of 1714 shows that a double row of cypresses also once marked the boundary of the formal *giardino all'italiana*. Its separation from the wild regions of the *boschetto* and cliff beyond was further reinforced by a high fence running across the whole breadth of the garden at the foot of the slope.

The lusty growth of the Giusti cypresses has often been remarked upon, although they have suggested different things to different people. In 1739 the French scholar and politician Charles de Brosses noted that, 'The great quantity of prodigiously high and pointed cypresses with which the whole garden is planted form a strikingly original sight and lend it the air of one of those places where witches hold their sabbaths'. Perhaps de Brosses was still shaken after his experience in the labyrinth, where for a full hour he had wandered lost under the hot sun before his cries brought help. Volkamer shows it in its present location in the northeast section, its fiendishly difficult original layout as yet untouched by Trezza's simplifying zeal.

In an almost forgotten area of the garden to the west, there is a remnant of the old city wall which once supported the *cedraia* or lemon house. The lemon trees are still overwintered here, in simple wooden lean-to structures reached by a flight of steps. In a niche in the wall is a large Bacchus, his youthful, paunchy features stupefied by wine, his genitals covered by a grotesque goatskin that only emphasises the bestial nature of his nakedness. He looks off into the distance with a frankly lascivious gaze while a small carousing figure hangs on to his right leg. The cryptic inscription, in fine Roman lettering, translates as: 'O traveller be not afraid, for it is to Bacchus the lover, not the warrior, as Genius Loci of this place, that this is dedicated by the master of the house'. Further along the wall is Venus, whose inscription reads: 'Without me nothing is fruitful, the statue in my honour

was placed in the garden so that Venus should live among beauty'. Of Ceres, who once occupied the third niche only the inscription remains: 'So that Venus not go without, Ceres is conjoined with Bacchus'. Wine, Love, Bread: a mutually dependent trio. It is a powerful reminder of the cyclical nature of life. Here, in a scattering of antique sculptural fragments and inscriptions, where gardeners have turned over the soil for five centuries, is a place where we can connect to our deepest origins.

From the belvedere at the garden's summit is a view down the tunnel of high cypresses, through the lovely wrought-iron gates and back to the entrance on the street. Beyond, all Verona is spread out to the southwest, her pink roofs tilting under the sky, her church belfries and medieval watchtowers rising to points above the horizon. John Ruskin, who described Verona as 'my dearest place in Italy', was moved to write:

> Now I do not think that there is any other rock in all the world, from which the places and monuments of so complex and deep a fragment of the history of its ages can be visible, as from this piece of crag, with its blue and prickly weeds. For you have thus beneath you at once, the birthplaces of Virgil and of Livy; the homes of Dante and Petrarch; and the source of the most sweet and pathetic inspiration of your own Shakespeare.

VILLA ALLEGRI ARVEDI
A CUZZANO
GREZZANA

THE IMPRESSION OF EXTRAORDINARY fertility is something not easily forgotten. It leaves a pulse in the memory, a sensation as of sharply indrawn breath. Villa Allegri Arvedi is above all a working farm – all tractors and revving engines, sprayers and muckspreaders, and there is the box parterre to prune as well. The place is immersed in a whirl of activity that involves the husbanding of apricots, cherries, persimmons, vines and olives, as well as of yew and box. Rising grandly on the western slopes of a wide valley that descends towards Verona, the villa is surrounded on all sides by the rhythmic contours of tilled land, each crop making its distinctive green pattern upon the landscape. As the hills rise in gentle mounds behind the villa's crown of white statues, the silvery haze of olive groves gives way gradually to the vivid green of rugged oak and hornbeam woods, guardians of the springs that have coaxed all this vigorous plant life into being.

In 1440 the fortified house at Cuzzano with its dovecotes, lands and garden, along with a stone lion contained therein, was summarily confiscated by the Venetian Republic from its owner, Alvise Dal Verme. He had been found guilty of lending his support to Filippo Maria Visconti, Duke of Milan, in that dynasty's continuing expansionist ambitions which threatened to upset the balance of power in northern Italy. Venice, which had received Verona into the republic in 1405, was implacable in her pursuit of perceived enemies and the traitor Dal Verme's former home was auctioned off to the highest bidder. It was at first bought by a Venetian nobleman, Andrea Dandolo, but by the turn of the

century it had passed into the hands of a Veronese family, the immensely wealthy Allegri.

By 1653 a flour mill had been added to the cluster of farm buildings that grew at the side of the villa to accommodate the various agricultural enterprises of the estate. In continuing expansion throughout the sixteenth century, Villa Allegri became an economic and political powerhouse, with an enterprising commercial outlook that it has

LEFT Club-wielding statues of Hercules stand guard at the gate leading into the parterre terrace below Villa Allegri Arvedi.
RIGHT New growth and old catches the brilliant morning light, throwing up contrasts in the various plant architectures.

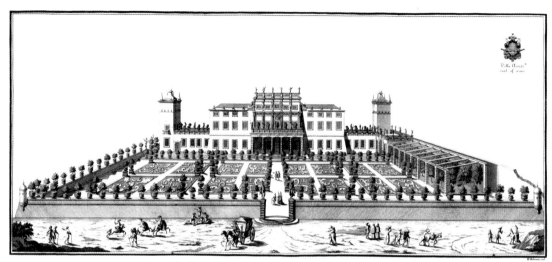

Il Palazzo, con il Giardino de SS.ri Conti Allegri in Cucciano.

maintained to the present day. By the early eighteenth century its collection of citrus plants was famous enough to be included in the set of engravings published in 1714 by the German botanist Johann Christoph Volkamer in his volume *Continuation der Nürnbergischen Hesperidum*. The production of citrus fruits was at this time a burgeoning horticultural sideline in villas all over the Veneto, and Volkamer's precise botanic studies of the many varieties of the newly introduced fruits were coupled with vignettes of the villas and gardens where he saw them growing during his travels in Italy. Just over a century later it was the turn of the silkworm to take the farming world by storm. By then Villa Allegri had been bought by Count Giovanni Antonio Arvedi who had plans to convert the building into a state-of-the-art mill for spinning and weaving silk. His plans never came to fruition but a large collection of copper stencils for printing silks still hang on a wall inside the villa.

The magnificent terrace laid out as a *parterre de broderie* that constitutes the garden of Villa Allegri Arvedi was originally created during the extensive enlargement and rebuilding of the villa which got underway in 1656. The Allegri brothers chose Giovanni Battista Bianchi (1631–87), a young architect from Verona, to give the existing building an appearance that would reflect the family's prestige and express their proud ownership of the expanding estate. Bianchi, who had trained as a sculptor, extended the house on either side and added a central portico that projects from the façade, creating a spacious balcony on

the *piano nobile* which is accessible from the sumptuously decorated ballroom. The view from here is meant to be extraordinary, and it is, for the elevation makes it possible to see the arrangement of the parterre, laid out on the flat raised garden below, to its best advantage. The curlicue and scroll patterns of low box hedges are cadenced by huge and ancient rounded cones and cylinders of clipped box and cypress. Beyond the retaining wall more topiary along the drive descending towards the gate emphasises the central axis. Two ancient cypresses mark the point on the perimeter wall where the axis once ended, a few metres to the left of the present gatehouse.

Undoubtedly the view across the parterre and over the valley to the hill opposite, with its similar patchwork of arable fields, vines, olive groves and the occasional copse, is beautiful, but what is remarkable is how appropriate the flamboyant baroque forms seem in this landscape, as if they reflected some aspect of the fecund nature of the place. Some of the older box plants in the centre of the design date from the garden's inception in the latter half of the seventeenth century. A comparison of today's unified design with the various layouts of the eighteenth century, known from drawings and from a fresco inside the villa, shows that it underwent modifications over the years, as

ABOVE This 1714 engraving by J. C. Volkamer provides precious testimony of the former appearance of the garden.
RIGHT A *tapis vert* leads the eye down the central axis of the garden onto the approach drive and towards the hills beyond.

PREVIOUS PAGE The majestic Villa Allegri Arvedi is an imposing
presence, overlooking the vineyards of the Valpantena.
BELOW Coloured gravel intensifies the decorative effect of the complex
patterns of scrollwork box parterre.
RIGHT Traces of the lemon houses are still visible in the masonry of
the high, south-facing wall enclosing one side of the parterre garden.

garden fashions came and went. The earliest version,
by Volkamer, shows sixteen square beds, each containing
curving, arabesque patterns, symmetrically laid out on
either side of a central path. Pots of citrus are ranged
along the retaining walls and at various junctions on the
paths. Such a plethora of box was not appreciated or
even approved by everybody. As a plant it attracted its fair
share of criticism for what the English writer on country
life Gervase Markham (c.1568–1637) had described as its
'naughty smell', while the French anatomist and writer on
agriculture, Charles Estienne (1604–64) even claimed that

its fetid odour so corrupted the air that it could kill bees. But as an evergreen and hardy provider of a multitude of shapes and subtle colour tonalities, box was unbeatable. Besides which, nobody was supposed to actually come into contact with it, since it was designed to be seen from a high vantage point such as a viewing terrace or window, from the comfort of the house. The oval pool and fountain were probably added at some time after 1719, when additional water sources were piped to the villa.

The extra water may also have been needed for the grotto that closes off the northern end of the top terrace. Partly dug out of the hillside, this airy, cavernous space adjoining the summer wing of the villa originally formed a continuously colonnaded structure with the sizeable lemon houses that extended down the south-facing garden wall. One side of the grotto gives onto an aviary where there are still traces of the frescoed foliage and exotic birds that originally covered it. An azure sky with billowing clouds once stretched up to a pavilion-shaped roof that was open to the real sky. Birdsong and the refreshing plash

of running water from drinking fountains would have formed the aural backdrop to the cool, vaulted hall with its three stalactite-covered niches. Much of the mosaic decoration that once covered the interior has unfortunately been lost. The remaining fragments, picked out in black, rust and ivory-coloured tesserae, show a variety of grotesque figures such as mythical beasts, birds and monkeys swinging on chains, leading some historians to suggest that the unifying theme may have been the mythical garden of the Hesperides.

Sculptures of Hercules occupy the side niches: on the right he is draped in the Nemean lion's skin (symbolising his first labour), leading Cerberus out of the underworld (the twelfth labour); on the left, a slack-muscled Hercules is shown dying from the effects of a poisoned cloak, given him by his wife Deianira, who had been tricked by the centaur Nessus into dipping it into a deadly potion. In the central niche, a gaping dragon contorts itself on the rim of a clam-shaped basin. He is Ladon, the serpent-like monster that guarded the golden apples of the Hesperides,

and that Hercules slew in his eleventh labour. Aside from the more obvious moral symbolism of Hercules triumphing over wrong, such a reference to the myth of the golden apples of the Hesperides was appropriate for Villa Arvedi, given its pre-eminence in citrus fruit cultivation. According to the many versions of this myth, the Hesperides were three nymphs who tended a fabulous garden at the western end of the earth. They were the custodians of a tree bearing golden fruits (sometimes referred to as apples), given as a wedding gift by Gaia to the goddess Hera, who also set the never-sleeping Ladon to guard the tree. The humanist poet Giovanni Pontano was the first to make a poetic association between the golden fruits of myth and the citron fruit in his *De hortis Hesperidum* of 1501, in which a retelling and partial re-invention of the Hesperidus myth is followed by a

disquisition on citron growing methods. Later botanical authors, such as Giovan Battista Ferrari in his taxonomic work *Hesperides* of 1646, consolidated this poetic tradition by classifying the major citrus groups – the citron, the lemon, and the orange – under the names of the three nymphs Aegle, Arethusa and Hesperia respectively. It was to such works, with their co-mingling of ancient myth and the emergent science of botany, that Volkamer was referring in the title of his series of citrus engravings mentioned above.

Water tricks were once concealed in the floor, studded all over with smooth, shiny pebbles like the bed of a stream. But the only water tricks now are the ultramarine glints of the modern swimming pool that has discreetly replaced the *limonaia* where the blossoms of oranges and lemons used to scent the air.

GIARDINO DI POJEGA, VILLA RIZZARDI

NEGRAR

THE STORY OF THIS GARDEN BEGINS WITH wine. Valpolicella is a mainly hilly region lying to the north west of Verona, sheltered from the north by the Lessini mountains and bounded on the west and south by the Adige river. The huge expanse of Lake Garda's southern tip lies just a few kilometres west, its deep waters creating a microclimate that keeps winter temperatures so mild that around it the vegetation is more Mediterranean than pre-Alpine, with maquis and scrub oak growing on uncultivated ground. The climate and soil provide ideal growing conditions for vines and olives, as well as stone fruits such as cherries and peaches. In Roman times the production of wine contributed to a flourishing economy, and mosaic remains at Negrar suggest that already two millennia ago this was an area favoured by the ruling elite for building their country villas.

The Rizzardi family bought the large estate of Pojega in the seventeenth century and established a tradition of winemaking that has continued, uninterrupted, to the present day. The clay soils and fresh climate produce red grape varieties used in the production of the renowned Amarone as well as of Valpolicella. In 1783 Count Antonio Rizzardi decided that the time was ripe to celebrate his family's achievements in a large garden behind the modest villa that sat at the heart of their possessions, surrounded by the rippling slopes of vineyards that had made their fortune. Not until almost a century later was the villa enlarged and given the vague appearance of an early Renaissance Venetian palazzo.

The architect chosen for the landscaping, Luigi Trezza (1752–1823), had originally qualified as an engineer of public works at the age of nineteen, but had since dedicated himself to the study and practice of architecture, training with the Veronese neoclassical architect Adriano Cristofoli. Cristofoli was close to the learned, aristocratic circles of Alessandro Pompei (1705–72) and Girolamo Dal Pozzo (1718–1800), both of whom were part of a consolidated Veneto tradition of gentlemen architects. Girolamo Dal Pozzo had completed the garden at Trissino following the death of Francesco Muttoni (see pages 194–201). As a result of their friendship, Trezza was introduced to the Veronese cultural milieu that earlier in the century had grown around the celebrated figure of Scipione Maffei (1675–1755), a versatile historian and playwright who, influenced by his travels to England and Holland, had begun to challenge Venice's oligarchic system of government. The reformist catholic approach advocated by Maffei did much to prepare the ground in northern Italy for the introduction of the enlightenment ideas that were spreading throughout Europe.

By 1783 Trezza was an established architect who had worked on ecclesiastical buildings and various country villas for the Veronese nobility. The garden he designed for Villa Carli (later Carli Cagnoli) at Oppeana was described by Giambattista Da Persico in his *Descrizione di Verona e della sua Provincia* (Verona, 1821) as containing a belvedere, plantations, fragments of antique sculptures, *boschetti* and avenues. Nothing is left of this garden, while the only other garden intervention by Trezza that survives is the simplified labyrinth for Giardino Giusti in Verona (see page 158). At the Biblioteca Civica of Verona, to which Trezza left all his manuscripts, books and drawings, are preserved the drawings for the four principal architectural elements of the garden of Pojega: the oval pool, the belvedere, the green theatre and the circular temple. Tellingly, perhaps, no plan of the garden exists, suggesting that the architect did not conceive it as a unitary whole,

The steep terraces of the secret garden to the side of Villa Rizzardi are linked by water flowing down a series of spouts and basins from the grotto.

but rather as a series of architectural episodes in which the visitor was led from place to place by following the strong hints provided by a series of visual axes formed by carefully planted and pruned trees.

In fact the garden is a strange hybrid, created at the very end of a century in which the geometrical regularity and symmetry of French and Italian garden modes were beginning, in the context of social and historical developments, to look reactionary and old fashioned, and it is often cited as the last example in the long and noble history of the *giardino all'italiana*. In northern Europe, topiary and parterre were increasingly being replaced, or at least combined with, the more informal, natural style of landscape gardening promoted in England by William Kent and later by Lancelot 'Capability' Brown. In the

Veneto, such ideas were slow to penetrate and the reaction was more conflicted than in neighbouring Lombardy, for example. One of the most vociferous opponents of the *giardino all'inglese* was the Veronese poet Ippolito Pindemonte (1783–1858). In 1792 Pindemonte was invited by the Academy of Sciences, Letters and Arts of Padua to present his ideas on the subject, formulated in a treatise that was not published until 1817, after political stability had been re-established under Austrian rule. In this influential paper he argued that the basic naturalistic premise of the English landscape garden was anyway based on the Italian poetic tradition, and specifically on Torquato Tasso's invention of the garden of Armida in his epic poem *Jerusalem Delivered* (published in 1581).

Notwithstanding such resistance, it is perhaps possible to see at Pojega the first concessions to the emergence of a new garden tradition. Trezza left the sloping site in its natural state, making minimal effort to impose the kind of terracing that is instead evident in the secret garden to the side of the villa, or in the area next to it surrounding the oval pool. Here, steep flights of steps, high retaining walls and narrow paths between box hedges create a complex weave of evergreen and stone, furnished by those equally

FAR LEFT The hornbeam avenue. A right turn leads into a perpendicular cypress avenue that proceeds uphill to the belvedere.
LEFT Cylinders of golden yew topiary in the lower garden. The bridge connecting the secret garden to the villa's first floor is visible at the top right.
BELOW Former lemon houses look out over a hanging terrace of box parterre. The central cypress avenue departs from the gap between them.

eternal elements of Italian tradition: water and sculpture. Around the pool with its central sculptural group of Triton, a new hedge of bay laurel has recently been planted, restoring Trezza's original design, while the *limonaie* overlooking it, originally built to house the garden's lemon trees, have now been converted into open pavilions for wine tasting. The secret garden, which is thought to predate Trezza's intervention, contains a grotto still decorated with real stalactites and inhabited by a river god who has unfortunately acquired a new head.

The five-hectare, roughly rectangular area of garden that runs along the sloping hillside from the north side of the villa is divided longitudinally into three areas, each with a clearly defined character. From the back of the villa, leading on from the six parterre squares with fountains immediately adjacent to it, and continuing along the central axis of the villa, is a spectacular hop hornbeam (*Ostrya carpinifolia*) avenue. Instead of meeting in the middle, the arching branches are clipped in such a way as to leave a slit of sky running the whole length of the tunnel. This luminous strip of light is mirrored below by a *tapis vert* that stretches in a narrow line in the middle of the broad gravel avenue. The two bands of sky and grass meet at a single vanishing point in the distance and the effect is stunning.

The second, central section leads out from the former *limonaie* and consists of a long avenue of cypress trees that are pruned to accentuate their poker-like shape. A third area comprises the *boschetto* or small wood which is reached by way of a rustic hornbeam avenue that extends all the way from the rear of the old grotto along the topmost ridge of the sloping land. Thickly and informally planted with oak, hornbeam and yew, it is traversed by a winding path that leads past the lurking forms of wild beasts, luckily only of the sculpted variety, although their thick coats of moss make them strangely realistic in the greenish half-light. Dwarf palms appear somewhat incongruously in the underwood, heightening the atmosphere of

ABOVE Trezza's belvedere made use of both stone and green architectures and doubled as a musicians' gallery.
RIGHT The round temple interior. Count Antonio wanted his garden to 'contain secret corners such as those praised by poets and philosophers'.

exoticism and danger. In the centre of the wood stands a small round temple, open to the sky like the Pantheon, only here it is canopied over by the branches of surrounding trees. In Trezza's original plan this temple was entered from one of four small 'green' rooms formed of box and bay laurel that radiated out from it and were connected to the temple's interior by narrow corridors also formed of plants. The effect of arriving in the small circular space lit by the dappled green light filtering down through foliage would have been uplifting. Inside, the walls are decorated with polychromatic pebbles arranged in such a way as to trace columns and architectural orders around the four door openings and the four niches containing sculptures of Hercules, Venus, Diana and Minerva.

Two-thirds of the way down its length, the garden is crossed by a perpendicular axis of cypresses running up the hill from west to east, and ending at a raised, octagonal *belvedere* with a double ramp of steps. Since it is placed at the top of the slope, it gives an enchantingly clear view over the rolling vineyards to the distant hills beyond. The area furthest from the villa is occupied by a large *teatro di verzura*, or green theatre, which was only completed in 1796. The largest of its type in Italy, it was based on ancient Greek models and is constructed entirely of plants. Seven rows of clipped box hedge form the semicircular amphitheatre, which is enclosed by a high hedge of hornbeam, clipped to form niches for the statues of Greek divinities by Pietro Muttoni (1749–1813), son of the more famous Lorenzo (1720–78). The grassy stage is formed by a raised earth platform on either side of which three sets of cypress wings are planted, and the whole structure is surrounded by towering walls of mixed box and cypress. In 1853 the

priests of Negrar wrote to the Bishop of Verona to complain that the theatrical events given here were not always of a very moral character. Their urbane superior replied that if that was the case, then on no account should they attend them, or they would be punished with excommunication. It is not recorded how the country priests reacted to this warning. The theatre, however, is still in use and has a seating capacity, on chairs in the auditorium, of several hundred.

Count Antonio's was a garden to be walked around with a select company of friends, a green artifact primed, by means of its striking simplicity and the scale of its separate elements, to elicit wonder, surprise and admiration. It was also a garden in which to enjoy music: the architectural belvedere allowed magnificent views over the vineyards and surrounding valley, but also acted as a

natural amplifier; an instrument played there could (and still can) be heard clearly from the villa. The same acoustic prodigiousness is shared by the green theatre, which seems to have been placed in such a way as to exploit air currents carrying sound along the cypress avenue that forms the garden's main, central axis, and filling the whole garden with music. But it was perhaps, above all, a garden in which to enjoy the fruits of the surrounding vineyards and ancient cellars, where the good flavours of the earth were so ably distilled. In this, it remains true to its original purpose.

ABOVE The green theatre was the last of the garden features to be built and is placed at the farthest limit of the central cypress avenue.
RIGHT Clipped hornbeam, box and cypress surround one of the twelve Greek deities placed around the green walls of the *teatro di verzura*.

VICENZA

VILLA TRENTO DA SCHIO

COSTOZZA DI LONGARE

THE SOUTHEASTERN CORNER OF THE
Berici hills around the town of Costozza has been
quarried since antiquity for its soft and finely-
grained white stone, known as Vicenza or Costozza stone.
Freshly cut, it has the consistency of hard wood, making
it relatively easy to work and to shape into building stone
or carve into sculpture. This property, combined with its
ready availability and mellow, creamy tones, made it the
material of choice for architects and sculptors throughout
the region, whenever the economic conditions were ripe
for large-scale building or decorative programmes. A
useful by-product of this activity were the underground
quarries, or *còvoli*, that resulted: hollowed-out caves with
cool, constant temperatures that provided ideal conditions
for the storage of wine. They also formed natural, ready-
made prisons, in which the unfortunate inmates were
never without work, digging their cells ever deeper into
the earth. Thus, for one or the other reason, or perhaps
for both, the settlement around the foot of Monte Brosimo
came to be known as Costozza, deriving from the Latin
custodia, a place of safekeeping.

The area's economy had been characterised by the
production of wine and stone for many centuries before
the arrival of the Morlini family in the fifteenth century.
Adopting the name of Trento, their city of origin, they
began buying up land and experimenting with the introduction of new vines and fruit plantations. In his will of
1583, Francesco Trento was at pains to list the improvements he had made to his lands: he had planted orchards
and gardens, piped water from springs in order to supply
fish ponds, and transformed a steep, stony slope into a
garden that had acquired the name of Mount Parnassus.

Five ascending terraces, of differing heights and depths, are also lent a
distinctive character by the varied nature of their sculptural decoration.

Aviaries and enclosures for game ensured that these
'golden gardens of the Hesperides', as he called them,
conformed to the fashions of the time. Trento was especially
proud of a system he had devised for conducting air
currents from the underground caves into the various
villas on his property so that the even temperatures cooled
them in summer and warmed them in winter. These
isothermic systems, which were described in admiring
terms by Andrea Palladio in his architectural treatise
I quattro libri dell'architettura in 1570, are still in place
and may be sampled today in nearby Villa Eolia, now a
restaurant, which once formed part of Francesco Trento's
garden. The centrepiece of the building is the frescoed
dining room, constructed above a hollow space where
cooled air entering from a long underground tunnel that
emerges further up the mountain is collected and then
channelled through a stone grate to the room above.

From the first decades of the sixteenth century, the
Trento family played host to a series of illustrious
visitors including the poet Torquato Tasso (1544–95),
the humanist scholar and mentor of Palladio, Gian
Giorgio Trissino (1478–1550), and later, Galileo Galilei
(1564–1642). A measure of the wide-ranging nature of the
scholarly debate and intellectual exchange at Costozza is
provided in a letter from Trissino to the Bolognese scholar
and geographer Leandro Alberti (1479–1552), which
contains the first known description of a subterranean
species: the eyeless shrimp that inhabited Costozza's
underground pools. Palladio, who was also a guest,
described Costozza as 'a marvellous place on account
of the diligence with which the Trento, gentlemen of
Vicenza, have had their villas built'.

Set on a sheltered south-facing slope, the park
consisted of several villas belonging to various branches
of the family: three sat at the foot of the hill while Villa

the lower part of the premises to the sculptor Orazio Marinali (1643–1720). Marinali was the head of a highly organised family business that, between the seventeenth and eighteenth centuries, poured out prodigious numbers of high quality sculptural works for churches, villas and especially gardens in the Veneto. There could have been no better place to site a sculpture workshop than directly above a ready supply of the necessary raw materials. From an internal staircase, Marinali had access to the quarry of creamy white Pietra di Costozza stone, from which he and his collaborators sculpted a sizeable proportion of the garden statuary of the Veneto, including that of the garden of Villa da Schio below. Later, this workshop was incorporated into the villa and transformed into a grotto decorated with frescoes of ruins by Louis Dorigny (1654–1742) and sculptural allegories of the seasons by Marinali in niches carved out of the bare rock walls. The Museo Civico of Bassano del Grappa, the town where Marinali was born, conserves his 'Album del Marinali', a workshop catalogue that provides a fascinating glimpse into the working methods of a high-profile stonecutter's workshop

LEFT A loggia links the rear of the villa to the topmost terrace of the garden.
ABOVE The former grotto-workshop of Orazio Marinali is now an elegant room within the villino Garzadori.
RIGHT The statue of Neptune outside the deep, formerly spring-fed grotto that forms the most antique part of the garden.

Ca' Molina and the villa now known as Villa da Schio were built on sloping ground further up. The garden that we see today is a fragment of this large complex, which seems to have been planned and built around a natural spring emerging some way up the hill, at about the same height as the rear of the Villa da Schio slightly to its east. Transformed into a Grotto of Neptune, this focal point survives, albeit in a much reduced form: there are still traces of the stalagmites and the painted decoration that once enhanced the watery, subterranean setting beyond the entrance arch. A finely sculpted Neptune stands in full sunlight over the pool that juts out from the shadowy recess of his realm and its containing wall, though just recently the spring, and hence the propitiatory presence of a natural water source, has sadly and inexplicably been lost, and the water now comes from the mains supply.

The villino Garzadori, constructed in 1686, overlooks the whole complex from the northwestern corner near the church of San Mauro. It became known as the Grotto del Marinali after its owner, shortly after completion, offered

of the time. The album contains hundreds of drawings of statues, vases, pedestals, portals, mouldings and other sculptural decorations, assembled by Marinali for the use of the various craftsmen employed on his premises.

The first attempt to return the garden to something approaching its original layout was made in the late eighteenth century by Count Ottavio Trento. To him are owed the series of five terraces, each of a different height and depth, linked by means of a wide path and stone steps along a central axis. The idea behind this restoration was to create a perspectival garden in the *giardino all'italiana* style, but it was barely completed when the property changed hands and its new owner, Count Giovanni da Schio, began transforming it along the lines of the newly fashionable, informal English style. Over the next hundred years, it underwent a romantic overhaul: tall-growing species of trees such as horse chestnut and plane were planted in naturalistic groups and exotic specimens such as paulownia, cedar of Lebanon and magnolia were also introduced. At the same time, the garden was enlarged with the intention of unifying all three villas, Ca' Molina, Villa da Schio and the villino Garzadori, purchased in 1837. The last, radical restoration, however, dates to the 1930s, when Count Alvise da Schio eliminated many of the larger trees except for those growing in the area to the front of Villa da Schio. Basing his intervention on the architectural survey of the property originally commissioned by Ottavio Trento a century and a half earlier, he returned the terraced garden to something approaching its 1770 appearance. It was at this time that the sculptures by Marinali were rearranged and given their present collocation.

The entrance gates on the road are surmounted by two warriors displaying the coats of arms of the Trento and Ferramosca families, in commemoration of a marriage in 1700. Beyond, a gravel path lined by box leads up a central axis to a succession of stone steps that climb by irregular stages the lower slopes of the hill. The retaining walls of the terraces are thickly covered in ivy and Virginia creeper, a combination that provides a handsome backdrop for the many dynamic figures sculpted in deep relief that

stand on rusticated plinths on either side of the steps and are ranged along the walls of the upper terraces. Clipped box hedges are used as additional framing devices, guiding the eye of the onlooker ever onwards and upwards, towards the dark arch of Neptune's grotto. A row of pollarded limes on the top terrace defines the garden's limit.

Appropriately, the first flight of steps is guarded by two lions, the instantly recognisable symbol of Venice, under whose protection the lands of Vicenza had prospered since the early fifteenth century. Once safely past them, and approaching the second flight of steps, the visitor is confronted by two figures of a more welcoming sort. Possessing the strong characterisation typical of Orazio Marinali's style, they have been variously interpreted as representing hospitality, in the form of the elegant page on the right who is in the act of removing the lid from a pot, while the older man on the left is traditionally identified as a merchant, a reference perhaps to the commercial interests of the Trento family.

LEFT The fresh foliage of pollarded limes on the top belvedere terrace is complemented by variegated yellow iris.
RIGHT Dwarves were a fashionable eighteenth-century garden feature. This one, playing a wind instrument, may be a travelling musician.

Diana and Actaeon preside over the long flight of steps leading up to the next terrace, while two hunting dogs hesitate at the base. Diana's divine association with nature and hunting made her a popular subject for garden sculptural groups, providing the viewer with the opportunity to admire the naked female form while experiencing a frisson of danger at the thought of Actaeon's punishment for doing the same. Here, on the garden's central terrace, Diana has just stepped out of the water and half turns, with her hand raised in sudden alarm, while across the steps, Actaeon, dressed in hunting garb and with his quiver full of arrows, is surprised in the act of admiring

her but has not yet realised his terrible fate. To either side are smaller-scale figures of nymphs.

On the next terrace, the ramp of stone steps is interrupted by a niche set into an arch in the rustic retaining wall; it contains a marine goddess, Amphitrite, whose nipples once spouted water. One of the architectural curiosities of the garden is visible here, in the form of the rusticated stone pilasters framing the niche: one is cut at an obtuse angle and the other acute, in this way tricking us into seeing symmetry where there is none. In fact, the terrace with the grotto which is directly above here and which forms the oldest part of the garden is not square with the terraces below it, of more recent date, and the garden is not, as it appears at first, perfectly aligned. A double ramp of steps runs up invisibly on either side of Amphitrite to the next terrace, which is dominated by the Grotto of Neptune. From below, the association between these two figures is clearly made, since Neptune appears directly over the goddess's head. Both stand on a dolphin-like creature that thrashes around at their feet and twists its tail up to cover their genitals.

Various allegorical figures adorn the top of the wall, while persimmon trees share the expanse of lawn with Zephyr, his cheeks puffed out by the gentle wind that will encourage the growth of flowers brought by his bride Flora, opposite. Behind them, two shallow aviaries are set into the retaining wall on either side of the Grotto of Neptune. The topmost terrace, which once contained the lemon houses, is now a lime walk with very pleasing views over the whole garden and is reached by way of the staircase leading up to a loggia at the back of the main villa. Copies of six grotesque dwarves by Marinali representing 'mestieri', or trades, line the banisters on either side. Within the loggia, the lush growth of an aged *Ficus pumila* or creeping fig attests to the moderating effects of the isothermic air currents, and has mystified more than one visitor with its two distinct leaf types. Where the plant hugs the wall on its upward journey, the juvenile leaves are tiny and overlapping, while the adult leaves, carried on coarse, drooping stems, are instead large and glossy.

LEFT The sea goddess Amphitrite was persuaded by a dolphin to become the bride of Neptune. Formerly her breasts spurted jets of water.
RIGHT A flowering paulownia fills the air with delicate perfume while Apollo, crowned with laurel and plucking a lyre, stands with a nymph bearing flowers.

VILLA FRACANZAN
PIOVENE
ORGIANO

To the south of Vicenza the rounded contours of the Berici hills rise suddenly out of the intensively cultivated flood plain. Their lower slopes are mottled with the various greens, yellows and browns of small fields of maize or fodder crops, olive groves and undulating vineyards. In the clefts of valleys and on the summits, farmed land gives way to extensive areas of dense woodland of sweet chestnut, oak and hornbeam, the haunt of truffle hunters and mushroom pickers. Several small streams meet in the heart of these hills to form a torrent that flows south, running through the Val Liona which widens towards the plain. Along its course water-driven flour mills and ancient farmsteads testify to a centuries-old tradition of cereal growing and quiet industry. The landscape, which seems to have been spared the often gratuitous disfigurement to which most of the Veneto has been subjected over the last forty years, is a harmonious mixture of man-made and wild, giving the comforting impression of a truce agreed upon long ago. On the southernmost tip of the Berici, its back tucked into the hills of Monticello, is the small town of Orgiano, traversed by a road that rounds the base of the hill, slightly raised from the plain stretching before it in all directions. The elevated position is a reminder of a time before the wetlands were drained, and hazardous, mosquito-filled marshes occupied the now prosperous and fertile flatlands known as the Basso Vicentino.

The Fracanzan were a powerful family who had been invested by the Bishop of Vicenza with land and feudal rights at Orgiano in the early fourteenth century. Over the subsequent 400 years, they extended their hold on the territory by further investitures, by the purchase of more land and by marriages with rival families. Keeping a shrewd eye on agricultural developments and the vagaries of the market, they variously grew rice, vines, wheat and mulberry leaves for silkworms, while a not inconsiderable part of their fortune came from the growing of hemp for rope, a commodity for which Venice's shipbuilding industry ensured a ready market. By 1710, when Giovanni Battista Fracanzan inherited the vast property, the family's ambitions had outgrown the rustic courtyard in which they had amassed their riches. A new residence was called for that would be more in keeping with their status as overlords and give them the opportunity to indulge in the leisure pastimes favoured by the nobility elsewhere. One of Vicenza's leading architects was engaged to design a grand new villa with a garden. The outcome was a truly monumental complex that is unique both in its proportions and in its survival intact to the present day.

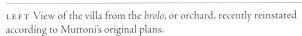

LEFT View of the villa from the *brolo*, or orchard, recently reinstated according to Muttoni's original plans.
RIGHT The four topiary yews in the gently terraced garden in front of the villa have been allowed to sprawl.

The architect Francesco Muttoni (1668–1747) had recently returned from Rome where he had been studying antique remains and taken part in archeological digs at the Colosseum and the Arch of Constantine. His visit was made partly in response to a commission from Lord Thomas Twisden for drawings of Roman antiquities and of buildings by Palladio. The English aristocrat belonged to an elite circle of neopalladians, gentlemen scholars whose rediscovery of Palladio's architecture was to have such an impact on English taste in landscape. Muttoni, who was born near Como, had trained in Vicenza and was deeply influenced by the older architect's works. He owned several unpublished drawings by Palladio and between 1740 and 1748 published a general edition of his works that included a reprint of *I quattro libri dell'architettura*, together with a commentary. During his time in Rome, however, he would also have seen Borromini's dynamic use of baroque forms in the many churches he built there.

Muttoni planned the new villa slightly to the west of the cluster of farm buildings that formed the nucleus of the Fracanzan property, leaving them to form the eastern boundary of a new, much bigger courtyard stretching out before a magnificent *barchessa* with twelve rusticated ashlar arches. This incorporated the scattered buildings that lined the bend in the road towards Orgiano's town centre. Unlike a Palladian *barchessa*, it is separate from the body of the villa and lies slightly oblique to it, perhaps more in keeping with the recommendations of the architect and theorist Vincenzo Scamozzi (1548–1616) who, writing some decades after Palladio, had opined that, contrary to his great predecessor's democratic ideals, owners might in fact prefer to live apart from the noise and distraction of their servants. Such detachment is also visible in the very great height of the villa, which sits next to the road on a slight slope at the base of the hill and presents a double façade, one facing north to a small amphitheatre cut out of the hills, and one facing south over the gardens.

The villa was designed to be accessed from the public road by a flight of steps that led over an arched bridge directly into the ballroom on the *piano nobile*. Crossing this huge room to the other side, the visitor would have been able to step out onto the loggia on the villa's south side and look out. The view was calculated to stun: beyond the low terrace with its formal garden and fountains was a mighty vista stretching along an avenue formed by double rows of hornbeam. One kilometre long, it thrust its way through space like a sword, disappearing on the horizon where an octagonal belvedere offered views in the opposite direction. A dark smudge of distant trees has replaced the belvedere and a pylon now imposes its aerial geometries on

the skyline, but the view is still breathtaking, unparalleled anywhere in the Veneto for its audacity and the forthright nature of its ostentation. Since the villa is only slightly elevated above the flat land, it was crucial for the creation of this view that the *piano nobile* be raised as high as possible and that nothing be allowed to obstruct it. To this end, Muttoni provided the ground floor of the villa with an unusually high ceiling, reflected on the exterior by a tall base of stucco-covered rusticated ashlar. The loggia itself extends upwards for two floors, above which is the huge granary for storing the season's harvest. Four separate flights of stairs within the villa ensured that the master and mistress of the house never collided with sack-carrying peasants.

The original four-part division of the parterre has been maintained, partly thanks to the survival of four topiary yews that have long since lost their pyramidal form and have been allowed to branch out into amorphous, dark shapes. Lines of box hedge have been replanted around them, bringing back a sense of order and symmetry. Two sets of wrought-iron gates set into the wall at the front and the rear of this area heighten the sense of separation between the different areas of the garden. A smaller version of the hunting enclosure, or *serraglio* as it was termed, already existed in the seventeenth century but was enormously expanded for the new villa. Nothing could have spoken more clearly of the enormous wealth of

the owners than this conspicuously large, walled expanse of cultivable land dedicated to the relatively unprofitable pastimes of hunting and fishing. Its forty hectares of open meadow and copse were filled with hares, peacocks, pheasants and deer. The two canals that drained the area were incorporated into the garden design as fish ponds, forming long orthogonal axes that intersected the imposing central axis. This began on the hill behind the villa, cut through the exedra and ran straight through the heart of the villa, out into the garden and down the majestic avenue with its enormous stone vases placed at regular intervals on plinths, almost as far as the eye could see.

The villa was sold by the Fracanzan family in the second half of the nineteenth century to the Piovene, in whose hands it remains, and it has naturally undergone many changes, as garden fashions and armies have come and gone. However, over the past twenty years, strenuous attempts have been made by the present owners to return the villa and gardens to their antique splendour.

The task of identifying and modifying those accretions from the garden's past which are unhistorical or unworthy is one that demands great sensitivity, not least because of its emotional implications. 'It was difficult for my wife,' explains Count Nicolò, 'to imagine the garden without the fussy bedding plants so beloved of her uncle and aunt. Her childhood memories are inextricably bound up with certain flowers that have since fallen firmly out of fashion, but should that mean that they no longer have a place here? They are as much a part of this garden, it could be argued, as the anglo-Chinese pagoda or the baroque fish ponds.'

Much of their effort has been dedicated to enhancing the agricultural and productive aspects of the complex, including the reinstatement of the *brolo*, or *pomarium* which lies to the west of the ex-parterre in its own walled enclosure. Stone steps descend from the formal garden into a long avenue of thuja, planted in the nineteenth century. The area retains its original division into nine modules, with the three on the left of the avenue dedicated to the growing of vegetables, and the six on the right to the orchards. Each module is defined by neat hedges of

LEFT An avenue of thuja in the western section of the garden has been left to age gracefully and casts an ethereal, silvery light.
ABOVE RIGHT Much of the garden is now dedicated to providing habitat for native fauna, but vines still have their place.

clipped box and contains rows of a single species of fruit tree: pear, quince, persimmon, almond, peach and apricot. Eating grapes grow on pergolas running between the partitions while figs have been relegated to the warmth of the low, south-facing wall which was formerly the home of the citrus collection. A second *barchessa* was to have lain across the north edge of this area but it was never built, and a *limonaia*, converted out of an old inn, takes its place. The citrus plants themselves have been moved to a less remote area of the garden and planted in the ground rather than in pots. Introduced to the villa gardens of the Veneto from the shores of Lake Garda, citrus plants rapidly established themselves as part of the repertoire of patrician gardens, their heavenly blossom and generous fruiting soon making them an indispensable element aesthetically as well as financially, for sale of the precious fruits made a considerable contribution to villa economy before large-scale commercial growing got underway in the south of Italy.

In the decidedly agricultural context of Orgiano, Muttoni supplied his client with multiple opportunities to entertain and impress his guests, not least of which was the exedra behind the villa, reached by a tunnel that runs beneath the road. Although his plans were only partially realised, this open-air theatre was nevertheless used for concerts and theatrical events, with the villa's façade providing a spectacular backdrop. The statues of the Four Seasons which adorn it are a fitting reminder, however, of how all this came to be. Elsewhere, stone inscriptions commemorate the improvements and enlargements made to the property by the Fracanzan, while others are dedicated in a propitiatory way to the pagan gods of agriculture, protectors of wine, fruit, grain and livestock. Scamozzi wrote that the larger and more spacious the garden, the more honour it bestowed on the house. He qualified his statement, however, with an observation that holds even more true today than it did in the seventeenth century: that the grounds must never be of such a size that they increase the owner's costs and make maintenance too laboursome for the gardener. The exedra is next in line for a long-overdue restoration.

VILLA TRISSINO MARZOTTO
TRISSINO

WHEN, IN 1404, THE CITY OF VICENZA was received into the Republic of Venice, the peaceful ceremony in St Mark's Square marked the end of long centuries of bloody strife. Fought over by successive waves of invaders, from the Ostrogoths to the Longobards, Franks and Magyars, the fertile lands of Vicenza had more recently been ruled by feudal lords whose shifting political alliances were imposed from strongholds such as the one at Trissino. Little outward trace remains of the castle-keep that once occupied this steep-sided crag dominating the Agno valley. Less than twenty kilometres from Vicenza as the crow flies, it was a well-defended lookout post that had served its owners well since the early Middle Ages. But having outlived its military purpose and with the prospect of more tranquil times to come, from the late fifteenth century onwards it was gradually transformed into an elegant villa.

The Trissino were originally German mercenaries who had made their fortune by controlling commercial routes in the surrounding valleys. There were various branches of the family in and around Vicenza: to one of these belonged the humanist poet and intellectual Gian Giorgio Trissino (1478–1550) who is credited with having recognised and encouraged the extraordinary talent of a young stonemason who was working on his villa at Cricoli. The young man was Andrea Palladio.

The irregularly shaped site with its varying levels and rocky outcrops posed a series of challenges for Francesco Muttoni, the architect engaged by Count Marcantonio Trissino early in the eighteenth century to convert his

fortress home into a villa surrounded by a garden. Born in 1668 in a village near Como, Muttoni established himself as an architect in Vicenza and in 1708 undertook a period of study in Rome, just as Andrea Palladio had done almost two centuries earlier. As befitted a student of Vicenza's greatest architect (Muttoni later wrote a treatise on Palladio), one of his main concerns at Trissino was how to unify the villa and its surroundings into a coherent whole in which each element related in a significant way to the others.

By exploiting to the full the awkward conformation of its hilltop position, Muttoni transformed the villa's plot of

LEFT A lichen-covered Charity stands on the edge of the octagonal fish pond below the lower villa Trissino.
RIGHT The view from the walled garden through an arch into the secret garden with its balconies suspended above a steep drop.

land into a garden that offered a series of quite different environments, all of which conformed to a common, guiding principle: the provision of various panoramic views over the surrounding countryside. To this end, his original designs included a large number of passages, walkways, stairways, ramps and even tunnels that led around the garden from one vista to the next. Some of these structures were completed after his death in 1747 twenty-five years later under the guiding hand of Girolamo Dal Pozzo (1718–1800), the architect who succeeded him, but most were never built.

The old square house, which still had not quite cast off its military associations if the battlements visible on a surveyor's drawing of 1711 are to be believed, had already undergone alterations and been added to in preceding centuries. From about 1722, Muttoni began extending it with a long wing that projected backwards from its north-west wall. Various smaller courtyards, dividing walls and a detached guest wing were demolished in order to make space for an immense quadrangular walled garden to the rear of the newly adjoining buildings, enclosed on one side by the new wing and partially on the other by the old house. A gentrified version of a castle courtyard, it is bounded by high stone walls running round three sides, the two shorter of which are perforated by a sequence of arches and windows through which the adjoining garden spaces are visible. Antique-inspired marble urns with carved reliefs are placed in the window arches, their

military subject matter sounding an echo of the castle's former life. To the south is the rear door of the older villa and glimpses of the entrance courtyard, while beyond the arches to the north is a secret garden with statues framing four curved balconies that project out above a steep drop. Tall trees now obscure the view from these, but from the northwest corner the foothills of the Alps are clearly visible, rising to snow-capped peaks in the near distance. It is a spectacular reminder of Trissino's strategic significance. The remaining side of the walled garden, running opposite the new wing of the villa, consists of a retaining wall built to disguise a stubborn outcrop of rock that Muttoni cleverly incorporated into his design by levelling the summit and converting it into a large hanging garden overlooking the courtyard. Access is by means of the nymphaeum hollowed out at the centre of the wall, from the back of which a spiral ramp leads to the upper level. In the original plan, this hanging garden was to have been planted right round with shady pergolas so that the fresh air and the magnificent views over the surrounding hills could be enjoyed in comfort.

LEFT The walled garden with the former castle block and Muttoni's additional wing. The walkway connects all four sides at first-floor level.
ABOVE To the north, beyond the secret garden, the distant peaks of the Alps are visible behind wooded foothills.
RIGHT One of the marble urns that decorate the courtyard, festooned by a single-petalled climbing rose. Behind, Winter pulls his cloak about him in the secret garden.

Neither this pergola nor the planned orchard with its 'various tender fruits' that was to have occupied this space were ever planted. But the structure built to link this area to the two lower levels where the *cedraie*, or lemon houses, were situated is still in use and has recently undergone a complete restoration. This is the little clock tower with a vaguely oriental air that stands at the southern end of the hanging garden and leads down to the lemon walk by means of a spiral ramp encased within it. There is a viewing terrace near the top and, like the tower in the Giardino Giusti in Verona, a window at every turn of the ramp gives views over the valley below. Another concealed spiral ramp on the northern side was designed for leading horses up from the secret garden so that they could be ridden on the large grassy space of

the hanging garden which, at some point after Muttoni's death, was transformed into a *cavallerizza*, or manège. The noble lord was spared the inconvenience of descending to the ground floor of the villa in order to practise equitation by the construction of an ingenious external walkway. This runs like a balcony from outside the back door of the first-floor drawing room, along either side of the villa's façade and then, turning onto the tops of the enclosing stone walls, proceeds between low balustrades to two mounting areas on the elevated ground opposite, levelled to be at the same height as the *piano nobile* of the villa.

One of the elements of the garden upon which Muttoni expended considerable painstaking effort was the junction between the pre-existing castle forecourt and the new areas of the walled garden and the panoramic avenue

area of the belvedere. Grass and weeds have invaded the spaces once filled by coloured gravel but the outline of the Trissino coat of arms, traced in curling scrolls of lichen-covered stone, is still visible. Lemon trees on plinths are scattered parsimoniously around and of the once large collection of statuary, only a few stragglers remain.

The panoramic terrace was once an avenue lined with cypresses, but the south-facing aspect of the retaining wall offered ideal sheltered conditions for the citrus collection that, by the eighteenth century, had become an essential part of the gentleman's garden. Traces of the old lemon houses are still visible in the stone niches high up on the wall where the roof timbers were slotted in, but the tender citrus have now been replaced by a spectacular mass of hardy climbing roses. The lemon trees are now wintered elsewhere but after the last frosts have passed they are still set out along this warm walk, interspersed by a fine series of statues by Orazio Marinali (1643–1720). Above, on a narrow terrace sandwiched between the two retaining walls, a long low greenhouse is concealed, containing all the plastic paraphernalia that the job of gardening now demands.

At the point where the avenue leads into the belvedere, four ancient cypresses stand sentinel, remnants of the former layout. To one side, a road winds down through the steeply sloping area of mature woodland that separates the upper from the lower villa Trissino, built around 1746 by the Trissino Riale, another branch of the same family, but subsequently incorporated into a single property by the Trissino Baston. The architect of the large, now derelict lower villa, is unknown, though it is thought likely that

where the lemon houses were situated. He finally settled for a design that articulated this difficult space by means of an extraordinarily ornate three-way gate consisting of rusticated pillars that frame three sets of wrought-iron gates. The left-hand gate leads up to the walled garden, the central gates give onto the lemon walk, while a third gate on the right was to have led onto a series of terraces on the steeply sloping hill beneath. Since the latter were never built, this gate now exists purely for the sake of symmetry, giving onto nothing more substantial than a sheer drop to the ground far below. Muttoni gave full rein to his inventiveness in the extravaganza of urns, pinnacles, volutes and scrolls that adorn the gateposts.

Naturally, the garden was also to have had fountains, one of which, according to a drawing of 1711, was to have formed the centrepiece of the octagonal belvedere constructed on a bluff at the end of the panoramic terrace where the lemon houses once stood. Its place has been taken by a circular bed of roses. A symmetrical pattern of finely sculpted interlacing stone borders covers the entire

Francesco Muttoni was at least in part responsible for its planning. The entrance gates to this lower villa, set at an oblique angle to the public highway that climbs up to the main entrance of the upper villa, bear all the hallmarks of Muttoni's style. Elegant and somewhat eccentric, their rococo flourishes of armour and flaming urns atop the gateposts distantly recall the Trissino family's military past, while the inclusion of wrought-iron *claires voies* as well as gates echoes Frigimelica's treatment of the boundary wall at Villa Pisani, completed two decades before.

Although positioned much lower on the hill, the villa nonetheless still commands a majestic view of the hills opposite. It overlooks an immense expanse of grass in the middle of which an octagonal fish pond mirrors the wide sky. Eight statues representing such enviable virtues as Self-dominion, Prudence and Magnanimous and Generous Daring rise above its greenish waters. More statues – thirty in all – gesture silently in the distance from plinths spaced around the balustraded perimeter. Behind them is a solemn backdrop of cypresses. The

statues, attributed to Marinali and his son-in-law Giacomo Cassetti, bear inscriptions that identify them as allegorical figures, gods and goddesses, and civic virtues. But even thus labelled, their meanings seem quickly to fade and be of no account, perhaps due to the absence of any discernible relationship between them, or perhaps because of the huge scale and lonely emptiness of the place. A double ramp of wide stone steps leads down to Neptune who presides over a dried-up spring and the fortieth statue, in a niche directly below the house, is a hunter with a dead hare.

The villa was damaged by fire in 1841, rebuilt, and then gutted by flames a second time shortly afterwards. The decision was made to leave the roofless burnt-out shell standing, as a sort of fashionable gothic folly. Its thick covering of ivy now enhances its air of mystery while a sharp note of nostalgia is introduced by the stone figures that decorate the balustrades on either side of the monumental staircase in front of the villa. Like tightrope walkers from a lost world they come, some playing instruments, some dancing, some in fancy dress and others bearing food for the table. They emerge from the encroaching woods as if obeying a long forgotten call to a feast that will never take place.

LEFT The exedra-shaped gateway leading to the lemon walk bears a plaque welcoming the visitor to a garden in which 'art is the friend of nature'.
ABOVE Scenes of Arcadia far above the Agno valley. A procession of musicians on the balustrade of the lower villa.
RIGHT Daphne's last struggle as she metamorphoses into a tree is outlined against the sky while two allegorical figures look elsewhere.

VILLA VALMARANA
AI NANI

EDITH WHARTON DESCRIBED THE GARDEN of Villa Valmarana ai Nani as 'a compositition of exceptional picturesqueness'. A hundred years have passed since her essay 'Villas of Venetia' was published and the intimate charm that she reported finding here – and which she observed to be so lacking in Palladio's country villas – still characterises this strip of ground extending on either side of the villa. From the outside, the villa itself is unremarkable, but its first owner, Giovanni Maria Bertolo, chose his site well. Within easy reach of the city, cooled by gentle breezes in the hot summer months and commanding magnificent views over the surrounding countryside, the

wooded slopes of Monte Berico had already been identified as a *locus amoenus* by Palladio, who in 1570 had built the last of his Roman temple-inspired villas on its southern tip for Bishop Paolo Almerico, a retired prelate. Villa Almerico La Capra, known as La Rotonda, perhaps Palladio's most famous creation, is a short walk away from Villa Valmarana ai Nani, along a rutted and seemingly forgotten country lane that runs between high stone walls. Bertolo, a lawyer and bibliophile from Vicenza, similarly wanted a place to which he could retire, far (but not too far) from the cares of a busy professional life, in order to dedicate his time to reading and study. The villa was built between 1665 and 1670.

LEFT Francesco Muttoni's classically-inspired loggia juts out from the *foresteria*, separating the garden from the stable block.

ABOVE The famous *nani*, or dwarves, look down on the world from their elevated position along the garden wall.

In 1715 the property was acquired by the Valmarana family who immediately set about enlarging it. By the standards of the day, the villa was not large, especially when guests came to stay, so Vicenza's most prominent architect Francesco Muttoni (1667–1747), already responsible for the design of Villa Francanzan Piovene (see pages 188–93) and Villa Trissino (see pages 194–201), was commissioned to design a *foresteria*, or guesthouse, just inside the main gate, with a new stable block adjacent to it. The villa's tympanum with its accompanying statues and the addition of a west wing to house an internal spiral staircase also date from this time. Giustino Valmarana's death in 1757 deprived him of the chance to see the decoration of his villa completed, although with great foresight, he had left payment in his will for just this eventuality. Earlier in the same year he had commissioned the prolific and very fashionable Venetian painter Giambattista Tiepolo (1696–1770) to paint scenes from his favourite works of classical and Renaissance literature, with a particular emphasis on the themes of heroic sacrifice and renunciation. Tiepolo leavened his depiction of the dramatic episodes of heartbreak and tragedy from the *Iliad*, the *Aeneid*, *Iphigenia at Aulis*, Ariosto's *Orlando Furioso* and Tasso's *Jerusalem Delivered* with luminous fresco colours and compositional virtuosity, bringing light and air into the relatively small rooms of the villa.

But it is in the frescoes painted by Giambattista's son Giandomenico Tiepolo (1727–1804) in the *foresteria* that a link with the spirit of the surrounding garden was forged. Although painted at the same time as the frescoes in the main villa, the subject matter is completely different: the solemnity and grandeur of noble deeds gives way to homely scenes of Veneto rural life, populated by characters drawn from all levels of contemporary society. It is perhaps possible to see parallels with the contemporary evolution of Venetian theatre in these painted interiors: the playwright Carlo Goldoni (1707–93), whose many comedies of the middle decades of the century poked gentle fun at Venetian

society, sketched its absurdities, its small-mindedness and its snobbery with a sparklingly witty and a sharply ironic pen. In Giandomenico's choice of subject matter, ranging from peasants to charlatans, merchants and masked carnival-goers, there is a similar curiosity and delight in portraying the sheer variety of humanity and the incidental detail of the everyday, together with a tendency to depict eccentricity in a manner bordering almost on the grotesque. The masked revellers are reminiscent of the stock characters of the *commedia dell'arte*, the improvised street theatre performed by travelling troupes of players that was particularly popular in Venice and upon whose traditions Goldoni himself built in the creation of a new theatrical style. Its comic effects relied on the burlesque interaction between fixed social and regional types who

LEFT A rural idyll. The Little Valley of Silence is visible from the terrace below the villa, here with a fountain and nineteenth-century well.
RIGHT Subtlety and irony are evident in this detail from Giandomenico Tiepolo's fresco 'The Charlatan' in the *foresteria*'s Carnival Room.

were characterised by wearing particular, often local, costumes and masks.

Giandomenico Tiepolo's interest in human types and in caricature, evidenced also in his drawings of a later period, is thought to have been the inspiration for the stone dwarves that were sculpted for the garden of Villa Valmarana in the second half of the eighteenth century. Seventeen of these survive and while there is no record of their original position, it is known that they owe their subsequent prominence on the boundary wall to the wife of Giustino's son Gaetano, Countess Elena Garzadori Valmarana, who is also credited with reorganising the garden. The famous dwarves face outwards towards the world at large, so that over the years the epithet 'ai Nani' (the dwarves) came to be attached to the villa's name. Carved out of the soft-white calcareous Vicenza stone, they are a curious mixture of ironic social commentary and grotesque caricature. Together they form a puppet-like repertory of characters or 'types', including the gallant, the doctor, the lawyer, the king, the Turk, the serving woman, and all are dressed in theatrical costumes with wigs, hats, breeches, turbans, heavy cloaks and the paned hose of the sixteenth century. The statues, some of which are

heavily weathered, have been attributed to a sculptor named Francesco Uliaco, and gave rise to a local legend concerning an unidentified daughter of the house who was surrounded by dwarf servants in order to prevent her from becoming aware that she was herself a small person. One day, she saw a handsome young prince of normal stature in the garden and fell in love with him but, realising the impossibility of her love ever being returned, threw herself out of a window of the villa. The versions vary as to why her servants should have subsequently found themselves turned to stone and banished to the garden wall, but they do not seem too horrified by their fate.

This legend, interestingly, recalls the custom in some European Renaissance courts of keeping dwarves and other physically deformed people as servants, jesters, fools and playmates. Some became treasured members of the court retinue: the status of the Duchess of Mantua's dwarf, for example, was acknowledged by her inclusion alongside her mistress in the Gonzaga family portrait by Andrea Mantegna (1431–1506) in the Camera degli Sposi in the Ducal Palace of Mantua. The short but powerful naked body of Morgante, a dwarf who lived at the court of Cosimo I de' Medici in Florence, was considered so exceptional as

to warrant his depiction in a double nude portrait – both front and rear view – by the eminent painter Agnolo Bronzino (1503–72) and in a three-dimensional bronze by the sculptor Giambologna (1529–1608), who placed him atop a dragon on a fountain ornament. According to the painter and artistic chronicler Giorgio Vasari, Morgante was in fact both a learned and a very kind man and his services to his master were rewarded by gifts of land and by being allowed to marry. But for the most part, these

people remained curiosities, exciting the much less noble but more usual feelings of horror and pity which were, however, more easily contained if the dwarf was merely a stone ornament. Sculpted stone dwarves became a popular feature of eighteenth-century gardens, along with characters from the *commedia dell'arte*, idealised peasants and various other human 'types'. It was a rare garden owner indeed who managed to keep them from creeping into some quiet corner of his patch over the centuries of their greatest popularity: even the august surroundings of Giardino Giusti in Verona did not escape the invasion, although they are easily overlooked by the visitor. But at ai Nani they are unusually numerous and prominent, lending an

LEFT The Veneto countryside enters the villa in Tiepolo's fresco of 'Peasants at rest' in the Room of the Rustic Scenes in the *foresteria*. Ditches bounded by pollarded willows are still a commonplace sight.
BELOW Villa Valmarana has the homely, domestic atmosphere of a family house.

air of whimsy to the simple elegance of the rose-filled formal garden that extends from the guesthouse to the front steps of the villa.

The villa's long and narrow garden runs along the backbone of a ridge bounded on the east by the garden wall, while to the west it drops to a lower, parallel terrace overlooking the so-called *Valletta del Silenzio* or Little Valley of Silence. Box topiary, yew and aromatic plants create a sense of intimacy and closeness in this secluded space, where, in late summer, three mature *Osmanthus fragrans* release their exquisitely sweet perfume into the warm air. Further down the slope, on a site now occupied by the kitchen garden, is a sheltered area where the lemon houses were situated in the past. A marble relief fountain is set into a freestanding wall once frescoed with architectural elements and around it mounds of playfully-shaped box have been arranged in a semicircle. No distant hum of traffic disturbs the peace; the only sound rising from the lush woods and patchwork of fields that dip and then ascend to the next ridge are birdsong and the tolling of bells from the Santuario di Monte Berico at the head of the valley.

The *Valletta del Silenzio* acquired its poetic name from a novel by Antonio Fogazzaro (1842–1911), *Piccolo mondo moderno*, published in 1901. A story of tormented love, it was the sequel to his earlier *Piccolo mondo antico*, and its setting was inspired by Villa Valmarana, in which Fogazzaro, who was married to Margherita Valmarana, lived for many years. The melancholy spirit of his writing is evoked most effectively in the woodland walk that continues southwards the longitudinal line of the garden beyond the stable block which was once the studio and living space of Carlo Scarpa (see pages 54–61). A forlorn sculpted St Sebastian is bound to a post among the beeches and oaks and a single tall column elevates a sculptured figure so far into the tree canopy that it is invisible. Further on, a Chinese pagoda with a brightly-painted exterior appears in a little clearing, a nineteenth-century addition that pays homage to the Chinese room painted in the *foresteria* by Giandomenico Tiepolo, and in perfect accordance with the Romantic mood prevailing in this informal corner of the garden.

LEFT Carlo Gozzi's *commedia dell'arte* play *Turandot* of 1762 may have inspired Tiepolo's frescoes in the Chinese Room.
ABOVE This Chinese pagoda in the grounds was a nineteenth-century addition to the wooded, 'English' style section of the garden.
RIGHT Wrought iron was widely used in Veneto gardens to fashion decorative yet sturdy gates, fences, and even ornamental plants.

GIARDINO JACQUARD AT SCHIO AND PARCO DI VILLA ROSSI AT SANTORSO

THE TWO NINETEENTH-CENTURY GARDEN creations in the towns of Schio and nearby Santorso were the result of a fruitful collaboration between one of Italy's earliest industrial pioneers and the architect he entrusted with the realisation of his philanthropic ideal of a worker's utopia. Alessandro Rossi (1819–98) was the son of Francesco Rossi, a shepherd-turned-entrepreneur who in 1817 had founded a wool mill in the town of Schio, north of Vicenza. Situated close to the high alpine plateau of Asiago, the town had for centuries been an important centre of wool production and weaving. A well-established cottage industry had been given a decisive boost in the early eighteenth century by Nicolò Tron, an enterprising Venetian noble and diplomat who, inspired by the technological innovations he had seen during his London ambassadorship, imported from England both the ideas and specialist workers needed to set up the first mechanised wool mills, first in Venice and then at Schio. Later, Tron's mills were bought by Alessandro Rossi, who took over his father's modest business in 1847, and in the space of two decades built it up into the biggest wool mill in Europe, employing over a thousand people.

As a well-educated and cultured industrialist-in-the-making, Rossi had been to inspect England's dark satanic mills for himself, taking a special interest in the model villages of New Lanark and Saltaire. He also visited Germany, France and Belgium to learn more about industrial processes and recent innovations in agriculture, both areas in which Italy lagged behind its northern European counterparts. It was apparent to him that his workers had undergone a violent cultural transformation and that in leaving behind their rural way of life for the town and the security of a wage, they had also relinquished their bonds, their support networks, the cyclical rhythm of a peasant existence, complete with its legends and superstitions. A liberal Catholic, he responded with 'enlightened paternalism', building a church, enlarging the hospital, providing childcare for infants, day schools for children and night schools for adults as well as founding a technical college in Vicenza and local institutions for the improvement of agriculture. In the New Workers' Quarter, a garden city laid out in the northwest of Schio in the 1880s, he built houses that were carefully differentiated according to social status and offered them for sale on good terms to his employees. In Rossi's all-encompassing vision of a perfect industrial society, there was little that he did not foresee or attempt to make provision for. He recognised also that, along with opportunities for recreation and entertainment such as sporting facilities, theatrical and musical events, his workers would be in need of something to replace the sense of magic and mystery, the experience of danger and perhaps even of beauty, offered by contact with nature. And what better than a garden to provide for this.

The site he chose, directly opposite the main gates of the 'Francesco Rossi 1817' factory, was already partially occupied by industrial buildings. A four-hectare, south-facing plot of land, it rises gently towards a steep incline

---

The courtyard, a pastiche of architectural styles, establishes a different time frame for the visit to the nymphaeum and grotto beyond.

at the rear, originally built over with drying sheds. In the first phase of the garden's creation, which concerned only the sloping area at the front, the wool warehouse on the east side was given an elegant façade and decorated with terracotta portrait busts of Schio worthies. Renamed the Jacquard Theatre in honour of the inventor of the revolutionary loom, it was converted in 1869 to house a theatre, library, night school and the gardener's house. Along the western boundary were weaving sheds, demolished in 1878 during the second phase of building and replaced with the small pavilion next to the entrance and additional island beds containing shrubs and trees surrounded by

meandering paths. Beyond the garden's northeastern boundary was the sixteenth-century church of San Rocco, access to which was carefully maintained by means of a path and steps, while the building itself was incorporated into the garden's scenography by the addition of a high bell tower with neo-Gothic decorative elements.

Rossi's close friend and collaborator Antonio Caregaro Negrin (1821–98) studied architecture and landscape in Venice at the Accademia di Belle Arti with Giuseppe Jappelli (see pages 102–10) and Francesco Bagnara (1784–1866), both of whom were protagonists in the development and propagation of the informal, 'English' mode of garden design in the Veneto. Caregaro Negrin developed an eclectic style in which he harmoniously combined elements that were in themselves quite diverse. His use of both native and exotic tree species together with the newest flower hybrids produced by a burgeoning nursery industry had its counterpart in the placing of architectural elements inspired both by local history and by traditions remote in time and place. The results were vivid, colourful, full of interest and surprise, yet tinged with melancholy. At Schio he added relief to the natural slope with raised, curving beds, some outlined by flowing lines of low box, in which were distributed prodigious numbers of flowering plants and shrubs, including rich collections of azaleas, rhododendrons, camellias and fuchsias. Groups of trees or single specimens were placed

so as to create a variety of views as the visitor moved around the garden, with the different heights and shapes of the foliage creating a picturesque and constantly changing scenery. The focal point was the graceful, curvilinear greenhouse containing Rossi's prized collection of orchids, its glass façade flanked by arches of red and yellow ochre while a long-gone statue of Flora stood on the terrace in front. On its west side is the most curious structure of the garden, a three-storey octagonal tower known as the *pisciatoj* which was originally a collecting house for the human urine used in fulling the wool. Artfully disguised as a dovecot or belvedere, it was left in place. To the side of it, steps lead up the steep slope to the belvedere walkway with its neo-Gothic parapet, and the atmosphere changes: the giant head of a crocodile, a homage to the waters of the Nile and the contribution of Egyptian civilisation to the art of weaving, projects from rugged rocks amongst which ferns and mosses grow. The path leads across the top of the garden through a succession of fake ruins that recall Schio's ancient castle, pulled down by Venice in 1512, in an all too realistically overgrown woodland where elder and ivy grow unchecked among evergreen exotics, including a Monterey cypress (*Cupressus macrocarpa*) and a giant sequoia (*Sequoiadendron giganteum*).

One can only imagine the wonder felt by people accustomed to the dust and noise of the looms all day as they explored this romantic garden created specifically for

ABOVE LEFT The *pisciatoj* with its oriental roof and heavy drapery appears well disguised in this 1864 lithograph from a specially commissioned *Album* by Carlo Matscheg.
LEFT The elegant curve of Caregaro Negrin's greenhouse, placed off-centre at the rear of the garden, conceals the entrance to the grottoes behind.
RIGHT A grinning crocodile head juts out from the damp foliage and rocks.

LEFT The near-derelict Villa Rossi at Santorso, as seen from the pond in the formal garden below. The roundels on the arcade celebrate trade and industry.
ABOVE A phrenological head remains in the dim interior of the grottoes in the Jacquard Garden, conceived by Rossi as a compendium of knowledge.

their use. It was, as Caregaro Negrin called it, a 'theatre of water and greenery' stocked with bizarre vegetable forms the like of which they had never seen: towering evergreens from faraway lands that bore no edible fruit, exotics such as palms and magnolias and the camphor tree, flowering shrubs such as oleander, tamarisk and forsythia planted solely for their colour or shape or perfume and not particularly useful for anything other than nectar for the loitering bee. A garden of delight and not of utility. Then, tucked away behind the greenhouse was another element of surprise: a nymphaeum entered by way of a fairytale courtyard with gothic arches picked out in a polychromatic mixture of stone, red brick and river pebbles and a monumental doorway crowned with a bust of the giant Atlas. Inside, airy vaulted interiors alternated with dark chasms and passageways studded with stalagmites and stalactites and crammed with curiosities and esoteric objects of every sort: a large phrenological bust and a stone dwarf are the sole survivors of this former didactic treasure trove, whose purpose was to lead the visitor on an ascendant journey through time and human history.

LEFT Villa Rossi's neo-Pompeian façade with two merino sheep
replacing the more usual (for the Veneto) lions of St Mark.
BELOW A merino sheep. Imported from Spain, the fine wool
of this breed was preferred to that of the coarser native breeds and
made Rossi's fortune.
RIGHT The *tempietto* interior contains an aquarium with its exterior
fish tank lit by natural light.

courtyard of this neo-Pompeian building and leads by way
of an underpass into a formal garden of clipped box with a
circular pond. Beyond this, on a wide strip of ground that
slopes down to the main road, is the extensive park where
Caregaro Negrin created a landscape of gently undulating
hillocks and hollows among which are planted clumps
and drifts of the native yew, downy oak, horse chestnut,
plane and beech, interspersed with exotic species such as
Himalayan pine, giant thuja and *Ginkgo biloba*. Glades
of mature trees create areas of fresh green shade among
the sunlit clearings, and everywhere there is the seething
sound of water gushing down from the mountain and
conducted, by means of a series of fast-flowing torrents,
rivulets and winding streams to the sinuous lake at the
bottom, where the uncanny root formations of swamp
cypress grip the muddy banks. Through a gothic arch,
where fragments of antique ornament are strewn casually
in the undergrowth, another doorway, this time Roman,
invites us, by way of descending steps, into the dim
interior of a circular *tempietto* with a domed roof.

The path terminated, by way of a precipitous stairway,
on the belvedere terrace above, from which there was
an unparalleled and auspicious view of the present time,
in the shape of the Lanificio Rossi and the industrial
town stretching out beyond it. A little to the east of this,
a dank and weed-filled cavity that is now off-limits is all
that is left of the ravine through which a waterfall, fed
by a cistern higher up the slope, came crashing down and,
by way of a little stream that babbled down the eastern
side of the garden, flowed under two footbridges to fill
the pond at the garden's entrance. Here, in 1899, a statue
in memory of the garden's founder was erected.

At Santorso, at the foot of Mount Summano further
up the valley, Rossi, now a senator of the newly unified Italy,
bought a large villa and in 1866 commissioned Caregaro
Negrin to enlarge it and create a private garden for his
own use. A double ramp of steps descends from the front

BELOW An antique-inspired stone bench with ornamental griffin.
RIGHT The lake, surrounded by an arboretum, lies at the foot of the
park. The bell tower of the Church of Sant'Orso, high on the slopes of
Monte Summano above both villa and park, was heightened in order
to complete the picturesque scene, and the trees planted in such a way
that its reflection is visible in the water.

Behind four thick glass panels set into the far wall is an
aquarium populated by ornamental carp. The statues
have been lost but much of the painted grotesque-style
decoration and some of the sculpted Roman heads in the
frieze remain. Elsewhere in the garden the exotic gives way
to the anthropomorphic, in the form of a 'Fawn's Grotto'.

At Rossi's behest the villa was turned into an
orphanage after his death and slowly fell into disrepair,
but the park, now grown to maturity, is a treasured
amenity offering botanical variety and the experience
of an 'improving' beauty of which Alessandro Rossi
would thoroughly have approved.

220

Visiting the Gardens

Almost all of the gardens featured in this book are open to the public for at least part of the year, but some are private homes, monasteries or hotels and may be visited by prior appointment only. The information given below was correct at the time of going to press, but it is advisable to check opening times, either by telephone or by consulting the relevant website, as these may vary depending on the time of year.

ISLAND OF SAN GIORGIO MAGGIORE
Guided tours only.
April to September: Saturdays and Sundays at 10am and every hour until 5pm
October to March: Saturdays and Sundays at 10am and every hour until 4pm
On weekdays, guided visits available only to groups of 12 and over
www.cini.it

THE EDEN GARDEN, Rio della Croce, Giudecca
Closed to the public.

CHURCH OF THE REDENTORE
Campo del SS Redentore, Giudecca 195
Enquiry at entrance to monastery, to the side of the church. Guided tour by prior arrangement and at discretion of the monk on duty.

BAUER PALLADIO HOTEL
Fondamenta Zitelle, Giudecca 33
Apply in person to reception desk.
Groups must make prior agreement.

CIPRIANI HOTEL, Giudecca 10
Apply in person to reception desk.
Groups must make prior agreement.

PALAZZO CAPPELLO MALIPIERO BARNABÒ
Campo San Samuele, San Marco
Private and normally closed to the public. However, guided visits are sometimes organised by the Wigwam Club Giardini Storici Venezia. For information, email: giardini.storici.venezia@gmail.com

PALAZZO SORANZO CAPPELLO
Rio Marin, Santa Croce 770
Groups must make formal request to Soprintendenza per i beni Architettonici e Paesaggistici per le Province di Venezia, Belluno, Padova e Treviso by fax: 041 2750288, or email: mbac-sbap-vebpt@mailcert.beniculturali.it.
Individuals as above, or by application to front desk and at discretion of concierge, Monday to Friday 9am–3pm. During the spring and summer months the garden often hosts exhibitions and cultural events during which entrance is unrestricted and different opening times may apply.

FONDAZIONE QUERINI STAMPALIA
Campo Santa Maria Formosa, Castello 5252
Tuesday to Sunday 10am–6pm
Closed Mondays
www.querinistampalia.it

VILLA PISANI
Via Doge Pisani, 7, Stra (VE)
October to March 9pm–5pm (4pm–5pm exit only)
April to September 8.30am–8pm (7pm–8pm exit only)
October 9pm–6pm (5pm–6pm exit only)
Closed Mondays and public holidays
www.villapisani.beniculturali.it

ORTO BOTANICO DI PADOVA
Via Orto Botanico, 15, Padua
April to October: open daily 9pm–1pm and 3pm–7pm
November to March 9am–1pm, closed Sundays
www.ortobotanico.unipd.it

VILLA BARBARIGO PIZZONI ARDEMANI, VALSANZIBIO
Via Diana, 2, Galzignano Terme (PD)
February to December 10am–1pm and 2pm–sunset
Sundays and public holidays continuously
www.valsanzibiogiardino.it

VILLA PISANI BOLOGNESI SCALABRIN
Via Roma, 25 – 19 – 31, Vescovana (PD)
1 April to 15 October 9am–12 noon and 1.30pm–5pm
16 October to 31 March 10am–12 noon and 2pm–4pm
www.villapisani.com

VILLA VALMARANA
(formerly Cittadella-Vigodarzere), Saonara (PD)
Visits only by prior appointment.
Information: 049 8790879
Guided visits organised from time to time throughout the year by Biblioteca Civica di Saonara. Check www.padovaeventi.net

VILLA EMO, Rivella, Monselice (PD)
Saturdays 2pm–7pm, Sundays and public holidays 10am–7pm
Open daily for groups by appointment only.
www.villaemo.it

CA' DOLFIN-MARCHIORI
Via Garibaldi, Lendinara (RO)
Guided visits organised from time to time throughout the year by local tourist office (IAT). Check website www.comune.lendinara.ro.it

VILLA BARBARO A MASER
Via Barbaro, 4, Maser (TV)
January and February: Saturdays and Sundays 11am–5pm
March: Tuesdays, Thursdays and Saturdays 10.30am–6pm, Sundays and national holidays 11am–6pm
April, May, June: Tuesday to Saturday 10am–6pm, Sundays and national holidays 11am–6pm
July, August: Tuesdays, Thursdays and Saturdays 10.30am–6pm, Sundays and national holidays 11am–6pm
September, October: Tuesday to Saturday 10am–6pm, Sundays and national holidays 11am–6pm
November, December: Saturdays, Sundays and national holidays 11am–5pm
Closed January 1 and 6, Easter Sunday, December 24, 25, 26. From 15 December to 18 January open to groups by appointment only.
www.villadimaser.it

VILLA DELLA TORRE
Via della Torre, 25, Fumane (VR)
Guided tours available by appointment only.
email: villadellatorre@allegrini.it
www.villadellatorre.it

GIARDINO GIUSTI
Via Giardino Giusti, 2, Verona
Summer: open daily 9am–8pm
Winter: open daily 9am–5pm

VILLA ALLEGRI ARVEDI
Cuzzano, Grezzano (VR)
Guided tours daily by appointment only, for groups of at least 10 people. www.villarvedi.it

GIARDINO DI POJEGA
Villa Rizzardi, Negrar (VR)
1 April to 31 October: Thursdays and Saturdays 3pm–7pm www.pojega.it

VILLA TRENTO DA SCHIO
Piazza G. da Schio, 4, Costozza di Longare (VI)
Tuesdays to Sundays 10am–6pm
Closed Mondays
www.costozza-villadaschio.it

VILLA FRACANZAN PIOVENE
Via San Francesco, 2, Orgiano (VI)
1 April to 31 October: Sundays and holidays 3pm–7pm
Summer closure: see website for dates
www.villafracanzanpiovene.com

VILLA TRISSINO MARZOTTO
Piazza Giangiorgio Trissino, 2, Trissino (VI)
Guided tours by appointment only.
www.villatrissinomarzotto.it

VILLA VALMARANA AI NANI
Stradella dei Nani, 8, (VI)
March to November: Tuesdays to Sundays 10am–12 noon and 3pm–6pm
November to January: Tuesdays and Thursdays 10am–12.30pm
Saturdays and Sundays 10am–12.30pm and 2.30pm–4.30pm
Closed January to March
Closed Mondays except by request
www.villavalmarana.com

GIARDINO JACQUARD
Via Pasubio, 148, Schio (VI)
May to October: first Sunday of every month 3.30pm–7pm
For information, email:
iat.schiovalleogra@provincia.vicenza.it
Check website for openings calendar
www.museialtovicentino.it

PARCO DI VILLA ROSSI
Via Santa Maria, Santorso (VI)
March to October: open Sundays
www.comune.santorso.vi.it

Further reading

James S. Ackerman, *The Villa: Form and Ideology of Country Houses*, Thames & Hudson, London, 1995

Nino Agostinetti, 'Giardini massonici dell'ottocento Veneto', http://www.pietrodabano.org/fileindexed/news/item/file0000016.pdf

Helena Attlee, *Italian Gardens, a Cultural History*, Frances Lincoln, London, 2006

Margherita Azzi Visentini, *L'orto botanico di Padova e il giardino veneto del Rinascimento*, Il Polifilo, Milan, 1984

Margherita Azzi Visentini (with Rosario Assunto), *Il giardino Veneto. Dal tardo medioevo al novecento*, Electa, Milan, 1988

Margherita Azzi Visentini (ed.), *Il Giardino Veneto, Storia e Conservazione*, Electa, Milan, 1988

Margherita Azzi Visentini, *Il giardino Veneto tra sette e ottocento e le sue fonti*, Il Polifilo, Milan, 1988

Margherita Azzi Visentini, *L'arte dei giardini. Scritti teorici e pratici dal XIV al XIX secolo*, Il Polifilo, Milan, 1999

Franco Barbieri, Guido Beltramini (eds), *Vincenzo Scamozzi 1548–1616*, Marsilio, Venice, 2003

Guido Beltramini and Howard Burns (eds), *Andrea Palladio e la villa veneta da Petrarca a Carlo Scarpa*, Marsilio, Venice, 2005

Vincenzo Cazzato (ed.), *La memoria, il tempo, la storia nel giardino italiano tra '800 e '900*, Istituto Poligrafico e Zecca dello Stato, Rome, 1999

Vincenzo Cazzato, Marcello Fagiolo, Maria Adriana Giusti (eds), *Atlante delle grotte e dei ninfei in Italia: Italia settentrionale, Umbria e Marche*, Electa, Milan, 2002

Annamaria Conforti Calcagni, *Bellissima è dunque la rosa. I giardini dalle signorie alla Serenissima*, Il Saggiatore, Milan, 2003

Thomas Coryat, *Coryat's Crudities* [1611], London, 1776

Mariapia Cunico, *Il giardino veneziano: la storia, l'architettura, la botanica*, Marsilio, Venice, 1989

Mariapia Cunico et al., *Nei giardini del Veneto*, Milan, 1996

Gino Damerini, *Giardini di Venezia*, Zanichelli Editore, Bologna, 1931

Mariagrazia Dammicco, *Venetian Gardens*, Flammarion, New York, 2007

Frederic Eden, *A Garden in Venice* 1903. Reprinted Frances Lincoln, London, 2003

Loris Fontana, *Valsanzibio*, Bertoncello, Cittadella, 1990

Veronica Franco, *Poems and Selected Letters*, ed. and trans. Ann Rosalind Jones and Margaret F. Rosenthal, University of Chicago Press, Chicago, 2007

Nicolò Giusti del Giardino, 'Il giardino e il Serraglio della Villa Fracanzan Piovene in Orgiano', in Giuliana Baldan Zenoni-Politeo and Antonella Pietrogrande (eds), *Il giardino e la memoria del mondo*, Leo Olschki, Florence, 2002

John Hall, 'The Garden of Eden in Venice' in *Hortus* 67, 2003

John Dixon Hunt (ed.), *The Italian Garden: Art, Design and Culture*, CUP, Cambridge, 1996

John Dixon Hunt, *The Venetian City Garden*, Birkhäuser, Basel, Boston Berlin, 2009

John Dixon Hunt, *A World of Gardens*, Reaktion Books, London, 2012

Henry James, *The Aspern Papers* [1888], Penguin Books, Harmondsworth, 1994

Henry James, *Italian Hours* [1909], Penguin Books, Harmondsworth, 1995

Enid Layard, Journal, http://www.browningguide.org/browningcircle.php

Georgina Masson, *Italian Gardens*, Thames & Hudson, London, 1961

Alessandro Minelli (ed.), *L'orto botanico di Padova 1545–1995*, Marsilio, Venice, 1995

John Julius Norwich, *A History of Venice*, Penguin Books, Harmondsworth, 1982

John Pemble, *Venice Rediscovered*, Clarendon Press, Oxford, 1995

Antonella Pietrogrande, 'Un'interpretazione veneta del nuovo giardino europeo: Selvaggiano, il ritiro campestre di Cesarotti', in Fabio Finotti (ed.), *Melchiorre Cesarotti e la trasformazione del paesaggio europeo*, EUT edizioni, Trieste, 2010

Francesco Pona, *Sileno*, Cierre Edizioni, Verona, 1999

John Prest, *The Garden of Eden*, Yale University Press, New Haven and London, 1981

Francesco Sansovino, *Venetia città nobilissima et singolare* [1581], with additions by Giustiniano Martinioni, ed. Lino Moretti, Venice, 1968

Margaret Symonds, *Days Spent on a Doge's Farm*, 1893, reprinted by The British Library, Historical Print Editions, London, 2011

G.F. Viviani (ed.), *La Villa nel Veronese*, BPV, Fiorini, Verona, 1975

G.F. Viviani, *Ville del Valpolicella*, 1983

Rosella Mamoli Zorzi (ed.), *In Venice and the Veneto with Henry James*, Supernova edizioni, Venice, 2005

Index

Frances Lincoln Limited
www.franceslincoln.com

The Gardens of Venice and the Veneto
Copyright © Frances Lincoln Limited 2013
Text copyright © Jenny Condie 2013
Photographs copyright © Alex Ramsay 2013
For other picture credits see this page.
First Frances Lincoln edition 2013

A catalogue record for this book is available
from the British Library.

ISBN 978-0-7112-3404-8

1 2 3 4 5 6 7 8 9

Commissioned and edited by Jane Crawley
Designed by Lewis Hallam Design

Printed and bound in China

CREDITS

The citation from the poem 'In Praise of Fumane,
the Villa Belonging to Count Marcantonio Della
Torre, Canon of Verona' (Capitolo 25, lines 307–21
and 484–89) is from *Veronica Franco. Poems and
Selected Letters*, translated and edited by Ann Rosalind
Jones and Margaret F. Rosenthal (Chicago University
Press, 1999). Reproduced with kind permission of
the publisher.

PAGE 28 Detail of Jacopo de' Barbari, Pianta di
Venezia, niv. CI CLIV n. 0057, reproduced with
the kind permission of the Museo Correr, Venice.
PAGE 81 Pietro Antonio Michiel, I cinque libri di
piante, It. II, 30 (-4864), f.98r., reproduced with
the kind permission of the Ministero per i Beni
e le Attività Culturali, Biblioteca Nazionale
Marciana, Venice.

HALF TITLE The Lion of St Mark, symbol of
Venice, the Eden Garden, Giudecca.
FRONTISPIECE Olympia and vases of citrus
at Villa Pisani, Stra.
CONTENTS The islands of Santa Maria della
Grazia and Sacca Sessola from the Giudecca.
ACKNOWLEDGEMENTS An imaginary landscape
by Paolo Veronese in Villa Barbaro a Maser.
PAGES 24–25 The Grand Canal from Palazzo
Cappello Malipiero Barnabò.
PAGES 62–63 Villa Pisani, Stra. The view towards
the stable block.
PAGES 74–75 Villa Barbarigo Pizzoni Ardemani,
Valsanzibio.
PAGES 120–21 Ca' Dolfin-Marchiori, Lendinara,
the isle of poetry.
PAGES 128–29 *Villa Barbaro*, detail of a fresco by
Paolo Veronese in Villa Barbaro a Maser.
PAGES 140–41 Villa Della Torre, Fumane.
PAGES 178–79 Villa Fracanzan Piovene, Orgiano.
BELOW Two herms on the façade of Villa
Pisani, Stra.